"Stephanie Winslow shares the pain and hopelessness she experienced as she lived through a much-loved family member's addiction. But she doesn't leave us there. She provides us assurance that, through the grace and mercy of Jesus Christ, we can leave fear and bondage behind and enter into a place of hope and peace."

—Colleen Conrad, director, Children's
Ministries Genesis Project

"Stephanie Winslow pours out her heart and soul in a very real, gripping account of how addiction takes hold of every life it touches. Her writing presents a desperately needed discussion and is a tool to equip those of us who are affected by the disease of addiction."

—Gene S. Whitehead, Christian writer and
blogger at *Simple Theology, Messy Life*

"In *Ascent to Hope*, Stephanie Winslow accurately depicts the painful journey in and out of despair that many of us travel as a result of a loved one's addiction. We didn't cause the addiction and we can't cure it. But amidst our grief and anguish, we can find peace for ourselves."

—Tom E., member, Al-Anon

"Stephanie Winslow's book reassured me that I'm not alone and that there is hope and healing from the effects of alcoholism. We are not anyone's savior, she reminds us, so we must turn the situation over to God—which isn't easy. But using her personal experience with addiction, she shows us, convinces us, that with repetition and practice, and by replacing negative thoughts with Scripture and prayer, we can begin to heal."

—Kathy H., member, Al-Anon

"The despair a family feels when it confronts addiction is both very real and life-changing. Stephanie Winslow's book shares the truth of that despair as well as the truth that faith in Christ can set free even those who are captive to addiction. Although often painful to read, this book will show you vividly and honestly how to navigate the nightmare of addiction."

—William Daniel Curnutt, retired chaplain,
Wichita, Kansas, Police Department

"If you have a loved one who is struggling with an addiction, Stephanie Winslow's story will give you hope and encouragement by pointing you to God and His great love. May your heart and mind become more whole as you read the honest account in *Ascent to Hope*!"

—Dale Fletcher, executive director,
Faith and Health Connection

"In *Ascent to Hope*, Stephanie Winslow describes with gut-level honesty her struggles to accept a loved one's addiction and find a path toward personal wellness. If addiction is an unwanted guest in your family, this book will affirm your fears and struggles as it guides you through a journey to hope."

—Randy Shuler, pastor and author of
*Hand Me a Dr. Pepper: A Fresh Look
at the Issue of Christians and Social Drinking*

"Stephanie Winslow has written a deeply compelling, heartfelt story that shows how prayer and faith in God can bring hope to a seemingly hopeless situation. Her book is an invaluable resource for churches, small groups, and individuals."

—Vince Burens, president and CEO,
Coalition for Christian Outreach

"As a licensed therapist for over twenty-five years, I found this book to be overflowing with insight and knowledge about alcoholism. Stephanie Winslow has nailed down the solution: recovery for the family is possible only through a relationship with the Lord Jesus Christ. *Ascent to Hope* is a must-read for all families struggling with alcoholism or other addictions."

—Susan Smead Balassi, MSW, LCSW

ASCENT
TO
HOPE

THE RUGGED CLIMB
FROM FEAR TO FAITH

To Jesus Christ,
my salvation, my hope, my all in all,
Who beckons me out of comfort
to reckless obedience.

For Christian Families Struggling with Addiction

ASCENT TO HOPE

THE RUGGED CLIMB FROM FEAR TO FAITH

BY
STEPHANIE WINSLOW

Stonebrook Publishing
Saint Louis, Missouri

A STONEBROOK PUBLISHING BOOK

Copyright © 2018 by Stephanie Winslow.
Edited by Nancy Erickson, The Book Professor®
TheBookProfessor.com

Scriptures marked AMP are taken from the AMPLIFIED® BIBLE, copyright © 1954, 1958, 1962, 1964, 1965, 1987 by the Lockman Foundation. Used by permission (www.Lockman.org).

Scriptures marked ESV are taken from THE HOLY BIBLE, ENGLISH STANDARD VERSION®, copyright © 2001 by Crossway, a publishing ministry of Good News Publishers. Used by permission.

Scriptures marked GW are taken from GOD'S WORD®, copyright © 1995 by God's Word to the Nations. Used by permission.

Scriptures marked KJV are taken from the KING JAMES VERSION, public domain.

Scriptures marked NIV are taken from THE HOLY BIBLE, NEW INTERNATIONAL VERSION®, copyright © 1973, 1978, 1984, 2011 by Biblica, Inc.™. Used by permission of Zondervan.

Scriptures marked NKJV are taken from NEW KING JAMES VERSION®, copyright © 1982 by Thomas Nelson, Inc. All rights reserved. Used by permission.

Scriptures marked NLT are taken from the HOLY BIBLE, NEW LIVING TRANSLATION, copyright © 1996, 2004, 2007 by Tyndale House Foundation. Used by permission of Tyndale House Publishers, Inc., Carol Stream, Illinois 60188.

Scriptures marked TLB are taken from THE LIVING BIBLE, copyright © 1971. Used by permission of Tyndale House Publishers, Inc., Carol Stream, Illinois 60188.

Scriptures marked TM are taken from THE MESSAGE: THE BIBLE IN CONTEMPORARY ENGLISH, copyright ©1993, 1994, 1995, 1996, 2000, 2001, 2002. Used by permission of NavPress Publishing Group.

Cover photo by Aila Images/Shutterstock.com

Library of Congress Control Number: 2018942235
ISBN: 978-1-7322767-0-3

www.stonebrookpublishing.net
PRINTED IN THE UNITED STATES OF AMERICA
10 9 8 7 6 5 4 3 2 1

"What a wonderful God we have—He is the Father of our Lord Jesus Christ, the source of every mercy, and the one who comforts and strengthens us in our hardships and trials. And why does He do this? So that when others are troubled, needing our sympathy and encouragement, we can pass on to them this same help and comfort God has given us."

2 Corinthians 1:3–4 (TLB)

THIS BOOK would not have been possible without the blessing of my brother who has been a friend, an encourager, and a source of laughter in my life over the years.

I am forever indebted to my parents, who instilled in me the belief that I can do anything I put my mind to, and that with God all things are possible. My maternal grandparents, Harold and Ruth, taught me more about living a life dedicated to Christ than I can give credit. My paternal grandparents, Ruby and Elmer, taught me to find joy in the simplicity of life and the importance of family bonds.

I would like to thank my dear friends Rochelle, Abbe, Kari, Courtney, and Kelly for pushing me to not be content with the status quo, and who have been incredible sisters in Christ.

Most importantly, I am grateful for the steadfast, unwavering support, love and encouragement of my husband, Marshall, and my daughters. My cup runneth over.

CONTENTS

INTRODUCTION   XV

PART 1: THE AVALANCHE   1

A LIFE UNDONE   3

THIRTY DAYS TO CHANGE A LIFE   11

RELAPSE   15

AN ADDICTION ALL MY OWN   19

24/7 EVANGELIST   23

SEARCHLIGHT CONFESSIONS   27

EMPTY EYES, HOLLOW HEART   31

LIABILITIES   35

PART 2: FROM FEAR'S GRIP   41

HOPELESS CAVERN   43

CONDEMNED   47

REMEDY FOR WHAT-IF   53

STAINS AND LABELS   59

FEARS RELEASED   65

PART 3: TO FAITH'S SUMMIT   69

BOUNDARY LINES LAID   71

IN GOOD HANDS   77

READY. SET. PRAY.   83

JOY LIKE A TREASURE   95

SOUL HEALING   101

GRATITUDE'S LEAD INTO ABSOLUTION   109

RECONCILIATION   115

DISCUSSION QUESTIONS   121

PART 1: THE AVALANCHE   121

PART 2: FROM FEAR'S GRIP   122

PART 3: TO FAITH'S SUMMIT   123

ABOUT THE AUTHOR   125

INTRODUCTION

THERE'S NO PRESCRIPTION or exact science for living life through pain and heartbreak. For the countless families I've talked to that have been plagued with addictions, every family has its own path to plow. It's not easy; I will never diminish the difficulty that addiction embodies. But what I will also not diminish is God's incredible power displayed through addiction, if we are open to receive it.

Much of my experience is as a family member of a person who struggles with addiction. I spent so much energy trying to fix and control what was outside of my ability and responsibility to fix or control. Talk about insanity. I spun in circles, in an effort to make heads or tails of what was happening in my life, and attempt after failed attempt made no difference. Sounds depressing. And it was a sad place to be in. Nearly ten years later, I have a new perspective. I have a new creed for my life.

God never promised me that life would be simple. He never promised me a picture-perfect life. He did promise that when trials come, He will be with me. With Him, I have hope. With Him, I have peace. With Him, I have freedom. With Him, fear fades.

If you are reading this book, you likely have countless stories of the times when you, too, tried to control every move the substance abuser in your life made. I'm sure you've cried yourself to sleep with anxiety over tomorrow. Perhaps you'd wake up, not knowing whether your loved one made it home or through the night. This is not a light topic or one that feels appropriate for dinner conversations. But we face a growing epidemic in our country of addictions of all kinds.

This book is the story of the hemorrhaging of my life. My hope is that as you read, you'll sense the pain I walked through so you might avoid my footsteps. My desire is that you also see the hope, peace, and freedom that have come to me through faith in Jesus Christ. Christ drained the venom of destruction that infiltrated my veins and breathed new life into my bones.

Oh, no! Oh, no! This can't be happening! This is not happening to me, not to my family!

I leaned into the apartment door to keep from dissolving into a puddle on the ground, one hand on the knocker.

Please, God, I can't handle this. It's just too much to bear. It's just too much!

I strained to take a deep breath and lifted the cold brass door knocker one last time. No strength left, it was a weak, faint knock. The brass tapped the metal plate. To my surprise, I heard the lock slide on the other side.

I jerked upright and straightened my clothes in an attempt to appear less disheveled and more confident. The door knob turned. The door opened.

I felt a rush of anxiety flood over me like a hot flash at what greeted my eyes. The man in the doorway, cowered and broken, said nothing but motioned me to enter.

PART 1
THE AVALANCHE

A LIFE UNDONE

S HE SAT, curled up, her arms wrapped tightly around her knees, chewing her lip as I rocked and nursed my newborn baby girl.

"She's a good sleeper?"

"Yes," I said. "We were fortunate with her. She slept through the night at two weeks."

She gnawed on her already short nails, her interest shifting from my daughter back to her worry.

"Hey, are you okay?" I asked. "Is everything okay between you and Luke?"

Her eyes would not meet mine.

"Yeah, why?"

"You've bitten your nails to the quick. Much longer and you won't have any nails left."

She peered out the window, her face flushed. Streaks of red on her neck revealed the anxiety she carried.

"He's an alcoholic," she blurted, as if in one more second she might explode.

I was confused. Who was she so distraught over? Her boss? Her dad? A friend?

"Wait—what? Who?"

"Your brother. My husband. That's who."

I stared at her.

"I don't understand. He likes a good party but—an alco . . . holic?"

It took work to form that word in my mouth. The word was foreign to me. The word rattled my mind.

My brother? The guy so securely perched on his pedestal at work and in the family? The guy who always has a joke, who's always entertaining, always the fun one to be around? The guy that probably half the guys I knew wanted to be like? He's what?

"No way. Not possible," I insisted.

"Have you noticed how he always carries a soda bottle in his hand? How frequently he goes out to the trunk of his car? Haven't you found it strange that he wears lots of cologne? What about the amount of breath mints and gum he uses?" Her tone was pleading. "He passes out on the couch each evening. Don't you see it? Please tell me I'm not crazy!"

"But I carry a water bottle everywhere I go."

As my words to defend him poured out, they were met with images of confused encounters. The smells I brushed off—*It's only mouthwash.* The frequent trips to his car, the bottle invariably gripped in one hand. They were all explainable.

Or were they? I sat, stunned, uncertain.

"I can't believe I didn't see it. I've been oblivious. The signs were there, but I ignored them."

We both sat and cried, slow and steady tears. She didn't have to convince me. I knew the truth. I just hadn't wanted it to be true.

"What should we do?" I asked. "Where do we go from here?"

Morgan shook her head.

"I'm not sure he'll get help on his own. I think we need an intervention. We need your parents' support on this also. Your dad's the only one of us who can pull it off."

"Mom and Dad know?"

She shrugged. "I tried to talk to your parents about my suspicions, but they got defensive. I'm sure they're in denial, which I understand. No one wants to believe it. I don't want to believe it either." She sighed. "But this is where we are."

"I can't imagine how they must feel."

"I need your help to talk to them. Can you help me?"

"Of course. Want me to call them tonight?"

She nodded. "If it's not too much to ask, that'd be great."

"Oh, Morgan, my heart's broken for you. I'm sorry you've had to deal with this alone and that we didn't want to face it."

I knew nothing of alcoholism aside from what I'd seen on TV shows and movies. What I did know was that the ramifications could be catastrophic. But Luke didn't fit the picture of an alcoholic, not the vision in our heads. He didn't fit the fall-over-drunk image. He functioned well. He held it together in public.

Later that night, after Morgan left, I called Mom and Dad. I needed to convince them a problem existed. We were fix-it people. We could figure this out. We just needed a plan to help him.

"Dad, I'm concerned about Luke. I don't want this to be true, but the signs are there, and it's clear we've done our best to turn a blind eye to them."

"Blind about what, Steph?"

The high-pitched buzz on the phone line filled the silence between us.

Bzzzz. Bzzzzzz. More silence.

I debated how to suggest our newfound reality. How do you tell a parent their child's an alcoholic? How could I say such words about my own flesh and blood?

Am I doing the right thing? Maybe I should hang up.

"Dad, you know he's got a problem with alcohol. It's serious. It's affecting his work—and his marriage."

Silence.

Oh crap, he's angry with me.

"Dad, are you still there?"

He cleared his throat and spoke.

"This time . . . with this . . . we don't know what to say, what to do, or how to help. It's all lost on us. Even where to start is unclear." He hesitated. "Your mom and I don't want this to be real."

My father always exhibited the strength to tackle problems, but now it sounded as if his customary strength had deserted him.

"It's not that we didn't know," he admitted. "We just didn't know what to do. I've tried to talk some sense into him, Steph, but I think that may have only made it worse, not better."

Dad carried more than the burden of a father. His was also the burden of boss, as CEO of the family business where we all worked together. The reputation of our family and the family business subjoined the complexity of this situation. I knew he felt beset with difficulties on many levels and stretched to know both how to parent and lead our family business well.

"Dad, will you please do me a favor?" I asked gently, trying to conceal the desperation I felt. "Will you call Morgan and talk to her? She has some ideas about how we can help to move this forward. Will you call her, please?"

"I'm glad you came to us, Steph. Yes, I'll call her."

"I'm really sad," I said. "I can't believe this is happening to us, to our family."

༄

DAD AND MORGAN arranged for us all to have dinner together. The plan included an intervention for Luke. Dad called with the details.

"Write a letter to him, if you can, and tell him whatever's in your heart," he suggested. "And please finish the letter with an invitation for him to accept help. We've worked to coordinate his arrival at an inpatient treatment facility. That should be all squared away by the time we meet for the intervention."

"What if he chooses not to get help? I mean, he will, right? But what if he doesn't want help? What if he's not ready for it?"

"I don't know. I guess that's his choice. All we can do is offer it and remind him how much we love him. It's his decision whether or not he goes."

The week crept by until, letters written, our hearts anxious and hopeful, intervention day arrived. It was a cold and dreary winter day.

My husband, Marshall, and I arrived early. Mom was cooking dinner. Her red eyes confirmed a week of tears and sleeplessness. Dad was pacing the floor. He bit his nails. He rehearsed what he would say. He wanted to get his words right in his mind before Luke arrived.

Her red eyes confirmed a week of tears and sleeplessness.

The wait felt long, not in duration but in depth of anxiety.

How would he take it? What condition would he be in when he arrived?

Ding, dong

Dad stood by the door, the handle in his right hand. We waited, but he didn't turn the knob. Instead, he leaned on the door with his left hand and prayed for strength.

The reality of what lay ahead for all of us was mere seconds away, on the other side of that door.

How much would our lives change after this event? What if Luke erupts in frustration and anger toward us all? What if he walks out and we never see him again?

The doorbell rang again. Anxious to do something, I swaddled Cora and walked to the back bedroom to lay her down for the night. Behind me, I heard the door creak as Dad opened it, followed by the rumble of voices and the usual niceties exchanged.

"Well, come on in," Dad said. "Your mom's in the kitchen, Marshall's in the office, and Steph is with Cora. Can I get you a drink? Iced tea? Lemonade?"

"Iced tea would be great," Luke said.

"Just water for me," said Morgan.

When I returned from the back bedroom, Dad called into the kitchen, "Bekki, we're all here."

I found a seat next to Luke on the couch. I reached over to squeeze his hand.

"Hey, buddy," I said. "Love you."

"Love you, too," he said with a puzzled grin.

Mom walked in and grabbed a tissue on her way.

"I'm not really sure where or how to start this conversation," Dad began. He looked up from his notes and made eye contact with each of us. "Luke, we're all here tonight because we love you very much. And we only want the best for you. We've witnessed the destruction that alcohol has caused in your life. We're concerned for you."

Luke looked startled.

"Each one of us has written a letter to share our love, thoughts, and hopes for you," Dad continued. "Is it all right with you if we read them now?"

Luke's eyes darted around the room without making contact with anyone. He reached for Morgan's hand and nodded, fidgeting.

"Steph, would you read your letter first?" Dad asked.

"Sure." I took a deep breath and slowly exhaled in an attempt to regain my composure. The paper in my hand shook slightly.

"Dear Luke, my big brother, I love you more than you will ever know. I have always looked up to you. I've been encouraged by the way you show compassion and care for others. You have such a big heart.

"Luke, I often reminisce about our drive together back and forth to high school. I knew you then. Today, your alcoholism has made you into someone unrecognizable. When we sit in meetings together, I worry about what you'll say. You often don't make sense, and you ask the same question over and over. You often look confused, like you aren't sure what happened. I find myself not inviting you to meetings you should be in because of these reasons."

I blinked to clear the tears that blurred the words I'd typed. Marshall handed me a tissue. "Now that we have Cora, I think back on our childhood and how influential our uncles were in our lives. I want Cora to have you in her life. I want her to know her uncle and to look up to him, to have an uncle who plays with her and makes her laugh. If you continue down this path, Cora will never know the wonderful, kind person you really are. My arms are open to you. I love you and always will, no matter what decision you make. My heart is broken because you're missing out on so much. Together, we can beat this disease. I will always be here for you. I'm here for you today because I don't want to see you hurt yourself anymore."

I looked at him. His eyes were glued to the floor as tears dripped from his face.

"Will you accept help today?"

He nodded and mouthed yes. We all cried, a mixture of despair and hope.

One by one, the rest of the family read their letters aloud to Luke. Again and again, the same question was posed: "Will you accept help today?" Each time he nodded.

Dad read his letter last. He concluded with the same question: "Will you accept help today?"

"Yes, I'll accept help."

YES!!

We leaped to our feet in celebration. We hugged him. We hugged each other. It had worked! Sighs of relief were heard all around the room.

After a few moments, Dad spoke.

"Morgan and I have made arrangements for you to go to a thirty-day inpatient treatment program. You leave tomorrow. You'll receive the help you need. Help is available to you. You just have to get on the airplane tomorrow and go."

Luke wiped away his tears with his shirtsleeve. He leaned over and hugged Morgan. She broke down, her relief evident.

Luke frowned. "What about work? And all of the customers? The employees?"

"We'll take care of it," Dad promised. "You only need to think about your health."

The next morning, Luke boarded a plane to enroll in the treatment program. We felt elated that he'd agreed to go. Finally, we could move forward. We dreamed of our old life: a life with Luke sober and healthy.

∽

I RECEIVED A COUPLE OF LETTERS from Luke while in treatment, the first written within days of his arrival.

Hope all is well with you at home. I've been progressing in my journey to stay sober now and throughout my life (one day at a time). I feel strong and excited about this wonderful opportunity, and thankful that you helped me get here. I love you all so very much.

In his letter he included an excerpt from the Alcoholics Anonymous *Twenty-Four Hours a Day* meditations book: *You must admit your helplessness before your prayer for help will be heard by God . . . It is not theological arguments that solve the problems of the questing soul, but the sincere cry of that soul to God for strength and the certainty of that soul that the cry will be heard and answered.*

Joy filled my heart as I read his letter.

Yes! He's got it! He's changed! He's back!

The note would come to symbolize his transformed life.

Addiction's like venom from a snake bite. It starts as a tiny bite, only a little prick, but before you know it, the whole body's eaten up with disease. It's not just the addict who is impacted so drastically; it's also their family and friends.

The disease spreads with its venomous effects and begins to hemorrhage every aspect of life.

> *Addiction's like venom from a snake bite. It starts as a tiny bite, only a little prick, but before you know it, the whole body's eaten up with disease.*

THIRTY DAYS TO
CHANGE A LIFE

THE SHORTEST DISTANCE between two points, we are taught, is a straight line. Life, however, doesn't always work like that. Life's a wonderful composition of paths, trails less taken, roads well traveled, and highways we wish we'd exited sooner. The journey, with its pit stops and restroom breaks, flat tires, and accidents, is chock-full of surprises and predicaments. With an addicted life, the hazards are frequent. Perspective on the journey is what makes the whole experience either tolerable, optimistic, or downright miserable.

Progress on the road to recovery is imperfect. But it still progresses. Perspective on imperfect progress sheds light on misguided hopes and unrealistic timelines. What we see with our eyes isn't all there is to the story. In fact, what's visible is only the tip of the iceberg, only a peek into what lies below the soul's surface in the spiritual realm.

Once Luke agreed to accept help and participate in the treatment program, we all breathed more easily. We thought, "Yep, now the worst is behind us, and we can all move on from this."

When he agreed to accept help, it energized him. He joked around and seemed at peace with the decision. Now everyone knew, and he knew everyone knew.

"Oh, Steph," Mom said afterward, "I'm so thankful for how this evening turned out. I hated planning it behind his back. It felt deceptive. I didn't know what to expect."

"I know, Mom. I didn't like it either. But I think we made a good choice for him, and for our family." I smiled. "It ended up a pretty nice evening with all of us together."

"Yes, it did! And thirty days isn't that long before we have him back. We'll get our old Luke back."

"I agree. I'm excited to see where he'll be then. A lot can happen in thirty days."

We left behind intervention night with its many turbulent emotions and took with us a whole new set of emotions, this time more positive ones. All our hopes were waged on a thirty-day recovery miracle. Check in: alcoholic; check out: back to normal.

The treatment facility offered family counsel and family education, which we opted out of, due to the distance involved. Our choice to stay away meant we could remain ignorant of the bleak recidivism statistics on rehabilitation centers: 50 to 90 percent of people who enter rehab relapse. Our decision not to participate in the family programs proved a detriment to our perception of the process.

All our hopes were waged on a thirty-day recovery miracle.

As a family, we ignored the facts and figures available. We anticipated a complete life transformation in thirty days. Thirty days may seem like a long time, but when compared to the years of alcoholism's stronghold, thirty days is nowhere near enough time to rebound. Our lack of preparedness illustrated our unfamiliarity, our incompetence with alcoholism.

One month of inpatient care isn't a panacea for alcoholism. It offers a good, solid foundation for a fresh restart but, in reality, it often takes several attempts to get sober. To stay sober is an act of God. After many such sobriety restarts, we learned to reset our perspective on what was probable and what was possible, and even what success looked like. An unrealistic timeline of progress, and a false picture of healing, bound us to broken expectations and failed results. Those failures became billboards and the progress nothing more than faded street signs. Time crept by while we waited, anticipating a good outcome.

God uses the patience required to refine us, like the refinement of metals. He skims off the impurities in our patience. He lives outside the realm of our finite time limits. Years are blinks of an eye to Him.

During the journey, and in its many starts and restarts toward a life of sobriety for Luke, we came to understand that progress, though imperfect, is still progress. We had to embrace the imperfect, to focus on the positive we did see, even if it looked minuscule. We also learned to celebrate imperfect progress and little victories. To celebrate involved a slowed-down life, a collection of hit-the-brakes moments to enable us to relish the beauty of each small victory.

RELAPSE

THE QUESTIONS FROM Luke's co-workers grew repetitive.

"Have you seen Luke?"

"Have you heard from Luke?"

"He was supposed to be on a call with me at nine o'clock. I can't get hold of him."

My answers grew equally repetitive.

"Sorry, no, I don't know. I haven't talked to him in a few days. I'm sure he had a good reason for missing the call."

These questions hit me like darts to my heart. I didn't know his whereabouts. But I knew enough to know he shouldn't be at work if he wasn't answering his calls.

I responded the only ways I knew how. I covered for him. I offered to help whomever was looking for him. I got involved in the phone calls and found ways to be invited to the meetings he missed so I could take notes and communicate with him about it when he resurfaced. I carried anger with me, anger at the treatment center for failing us and animosity toward him for not being strong enough to avoid these relapses. He hadn't returned "fixed."

One morning, no one had heard from him and he didn't return any calls. One too many people asked why. A horrible feeling came over me. I panicked.

This is it. He's dead.

I walked as calmly as I could to my husband's desk, anxious not to freak out in front of the entire staff.

"Marshall, I need to go over to Luke's apartment and check on him. No one's been able to reach him. I don't know—I have a bad feeling. Something's different this time."

"Do you need me to come with you?" he asked.

"No, I'll call you after I check on him."

I flew down the stairwell from the second-floor offices to the car. Taking a deep breath, I turned the key in the ignition. I exhaled raggedly, and the tears came.

Lord, please let him be alive. Father, please keep Your hand on him and protect him. Please, Lord, I don't want to lose him.

"Jesus . . . Jesus . . . Jesus . . ." I repeated this plea to comfort my scattered mind.

When I reached Luke's apartment building, I tore into the parking lot and sprang out of the car, on the mission of a lifetime.

He has to be home.

I dashed out of the elevator and sprinted down the long hallway. I couldn't catch my breath. My body radiated heat, yet my hands were cold as ice and clammy. My whole body trembled with fear. I banged on the door, my inner warrior slamming my fist against the door with everything I had.

No answer.

Lord, please let him be okay. Please let him answer.

I banged again, even more insistently.

Please, God.

Still no answer.

I leaned against the wall and slid to the floor, hugging my legs.

What do I do? I have to get in there.

As I was about to give up, I heard the lock click. The door cracked open, revealing a man, hunched over, wobbling slightly, whose eyes would not meet mine. It was the shell of a man that had once housed my brother. Despite my dismay, relief flooded my bones. A shell of a man, but alive.

He waved me in, silently, and turned and staggered inside, through the entryway and into the family room. I followed, equally silent. Anger, pain, brokenness, sadness, and grief—all these emotions rolled round and round, inside my broken heart.

I broke the silence.

"Luke, you have no idea how relieved I am that you answered that door. We couldn't get hold of you, and we were worried sick."

He crossed his arms, eyes downcast. He anchored his hip against the loveseat to secure his balance.

"I haven't seen you in a while. Where've you been? I barely recognize you." My voice rose in pitch, yet weaker as I strained to share the ache of my heart. "Please stop this. You're killing yourself! We're all so worried about you."

Expressionless, he stared at the floor.

"Don't you understand? You'll lose your job! Do you even care? You've hurt yourself. You've hurt us. Do you care?"

It was as if I hadn't spoken.

Maybe something I say will strike a chord with him. Maybe I can encourage him.

"You've gotta show up. You've gotta be the big brother. I need my brother. I miss our talks. I miss *you*. Please, Luke, say something." I pleaded.

No response.

Not knowing what else to say, I blurted, "I'm glad you're alive, even if you don't want to be." When he didn't react, I demanded, "Why won't you say something?"

In the quiet of the next moments, I realized we were in over our heads. Neither of us knew what *"I'm glad you're alive, even if you don't want to be."* to do now, where to go, who to turn to, or what to say next.

I stared into his dull, empty eyes. The glimmer was gone. I tried to convince myself I was in a bad dream, that I'd entered the wrong apartment. After all, he didn't look like Luke. He had become a stranger. Unrecognizable.

Would he have fallen this far, would he be this lost, if Morgan had chosen to stay and fight for him instead of leaving him?

In my heart I blamed her for his spiral deeper into addiction after she'd left him, though in my head I didn't blame her for leaving. It was a choice I would have made, too, if I had found myself in her shoes. Who could deal with the dramatic highs and lows on such an intimate, daily level? I wasn't strong enough to handle what I periodically encountered, let alone a daily dose.

Our eyes locked on each other. Still he said nothing.

His shoulders shook as he began to weep.

"I'm sorry. This is hard. I don't want to hurt you." I said, and reached out and hugged him.

He cried in my arms. I had no tears left. Alcoholism had beaten us into submission. The addiction approached the finish line, seemingly victorious.

"Can you please call the office?" I asked.

He wiped his tears from swollen, ancient eyes with aged hands.

"I'm sorry to have hurt you," he wheezed. "Sorry you had to see me like this." He hesitated. "Thank you for coming here. It means a lot."

I hugged him again.

"We're praying for you. Courage. Strength. God knows what you need. Trust Him," I urged. With that, I left.

On the ride back to the office, the silo of tears, believed to be exhausted, had somehow been replenished. With the radio turned up loud to praise and worship music, I melted into the seat. The silo doors unlocked, and the tears poured out.

I reflected on all that I'd said, and all that he hadn't said. The image of who he'd become haunted me. He was a haggard thirty-two-year-old man with the stooped posture of a ninety-year-old man. Broken body. Worn down. Defeated. The disease had taken him hostage.

Back at work, Marshall tracked me down.

"How are you? How'd it go?"

"My heart is wrecked," I said, as he drew me into his arms. "That person I saw, I don't know him. He looked like a ghost. Empty. Hollow. Lost."

He looked like a ghost.
Empty. Hollow. Lost.

"Oh, sweetie," he said, "I'm so sorry."

"I really thought we'd lost him."

"If he's breathing, Steph, there's still hope." Marshall said.

AN ADDICTION
ALL MY OWN

WHILE LUKE'S ADDICTION WORSENED, I developed an addiction all my own: an addiction to save him. The weight of all that surrounded me began to crush me. I had failed. I couldn't handle it. I buckled under the pressure to beat it.

Addiction took over every aspect of my life, including my relationships with my husband and children. The anger I felt toward God and the situation got the best of me most days. I couldn't see that Luke's salvation wasn't my job. I grew consumed, enamored even, by the idea that I could be the one to draw him back to Christ. My relationship with Marshall grew strained as I relied on him to be the backbone and emotional support for our two girls. Blowup after blowup. Mis-reactions and harsh words.

My life became unmanageable.

When the four of us were in the same room together, Marshall and the girls talked and giggled, while I poured all my attention into work, to what felt controllable. Wrapped in my own thoughts, I didn't hear the conversations. I blocked those sweet little voices and missed out on so much goodness—laughter, joy, and fun, all with the potential to lift my spirits. I ignored what would have otherwise brought me joy, relief, and a ray of hope. Worse yet, my children were led to believe that my thoughts held greater importance than whatever they wanted to say or show me.

"Mom . . . Mom? *Mom!*"

"Stephanie, Cora is trying to talk to you," Marshall said.

Silence.

"Steph, did you hear me? Cora wants to talk to you."

"What? Yes, yes, I hear you," I snapped. "Can't you see I'm in the middle of work here?"

"Sorry, Mommy," Cora mumbled.

"Come on, Steph, can't that wait?"

"No, it can't! This report has to be done tomorrow for the board meeting. If I don't do it, it won't get done. There's no one else to do it! There's no more time. I have to do it now."

"All right. Cora, you can tell Mom your story later, okay? She can put you to bed tonight, and you can tell her then."

"Okay, Daddy."

Worse yet, my children were led to believe that my thoughts held greater importance than whatever they wanted to say or show me.

Their voices barely registered. And just like that, one of the thousands of missed opportunities to stop and listen had passed by. No time could be made to be an ear, even just for a moment, for my little girls—no time given by me to show up and be their mom.

I never made a conscious effort to tune everything out; in fact, quite the opposite. Yet thoughtful attention to be a mental and emotional as well as a physical presence for my family required focused effort. Being in a room together and being present are different. The latter took concerted effort and intentionality.

Instead, it became easier to remain wrapped up in my thoughts: the plans, the schemes, the manipulations, and the solutions to save Luke. My inner thoughts, though cloudy, were easier to face than to come up for air and face all I had missed. I used work as a cover—smoke and mirrors—to avoid what I knew needed to be fixed. *I* needed to be fixed. My kids needed their mom. My husband needed his wife. My addiction to being Luke's fixer-upper fostered the birth of an absentee wife and parent.

My own addiction to save, to win, to beat alcoholism infected the most intimate relationships. No vacancy was available for any other considerations. Any other pain or conflict threatened to overwhelm me, so I pushed it all away. My interests were set on a solution to "fix" Luke and win against addiction. My addiction to win came at the expense of my husband and my kids.

Fear. Anxiety. Worry. Depression. Hopelessness. These feelings I knew well. And I knew Jesus. I already had the answers that I sought hard to find, but I ignored their existence. I didn't like the answers I'd gotten because it meant I had to be content with no solution.

How do people make it through the hopelessness of addiction without the cross of Christ? How can one be a good, loving, and present mom with all these emotions and thoughts whirling in one's mind and consuming one's very being? It's impossible when one is apart from Christ.

24/7 EVANGELIST

I BECAME Luke's personal evangelist, on call 24/7. My goal, throughout what would become a seven-year hiatus from sanity, was to ensure that he would make it to Heaven, that his salvation would be signed, sealed, and delivered. Worse yet, if he didn't, I was convinced it would be my fault. I doubted his salvation, even though we had sat together as children and memorized the same scripture, sang the same praise songs, and answered the same Bible trivia questions. My doubt led me into action as if his salvation were solely up to me.

Slow or no progress toward recovery sent me into a tailspin of cyclical half-truths or outright lies from Satan that tempted me to shoulder sole responsibility for Luke's salvation. The guilt spiral reeled. I didn't pray enough, invite enough, or speak truth and confront enough.

It was about me and my ability to "save." The irony grew to expose a kink in my faith's chain. I didn't ask, "Do I love enough?"

There was a period of about nine months where every day I would sit at my computer with my Bible and devotion books and search, scouring for verses to send him, verses to help him see the light. I wanted to encourage him to have a relationship with Christ. I wanted him to know that I was fighting for his life, and that I was on his side.

One evening I wrote, quoting Ephesians 6:13-16 (TM): "Today may you be reminded the Lord will help you. 'Be prepared. You're up against far more than you can handle on your own. Take all the help you can get, every weapon God has issued, so that when it's all over but the shouting you'll still be on your feet. Truth, righteousness, peace, faith, salvation are more than words. Learn how to apply them. You'll need them throughout your life. God's Word is an indispensable weapon. In the same way, prayer is essential in this ongoing warfare. Pray hard and long. Pray for your brothers and sisters. Keep your eyes open. Keep each other's spirits up so that no one falls behind or drops out.'

"You're in a battle, brother," I wrote. "You're in a war over your soul. Satan's attacking you with everything he has in his armory. You must choose if you're going to let God be your shield and your protection, so you'll be able to see victory and freedom in your life . . . I'm fighting for you. I pray every day that you come to know God in a new way and that He will rescue you from the chains that have you bound. I'll never give up on you. I'll never stop praying for you."

Nearly every day for nine months, I evangelized to Luke at every opportunity. Even with this intense focus, this intentionality to "save" him, nothing happened. He did not change. I felt doomed. And then it dawned on me that his ears were unable to hear anything I said because I didn't know his heart.

Salvation was not my responsibility, not even close to being within my power. I needed truth speakers in my life to help discern Satan's lies and recognize the traps—friends to illuminate the gaps in thought. Enlightenment moments with friends serve as a solid slap upside the head. One of these enlightenment moments happened at a coffee shop. There, a dear friend listened as I poured out my chronic perpetual worry.

"Maybe I should invite him to church this Sunday. I think he'd like the topic. Or maybe it'd be better to ask him to come with Marshall and me to the Casting Crowns concert? He really loves music. Maybe this'll be the weekend he surrenders. Maybe this'll be the weekend he decides he's sick and tired of being sick and tired. What do you think? Do you have any ideas, Kelly?"

She took a deep breath and stared into her cup of white chocolate mocha. Looking up, she reached over and took my hand, her caring, deep-brown eyes locked on mine.

"But Stephanie, this is not your cross to bear; this is not your burden to carry. That's why Jesus died. You carry what you've no business carrying." She shook her head. "I have no ideas for you. I can't tell you what you should do because you've done enough. Truth is, it's God's time. His plan. His purpose. His will."

As her words washed over me, my body awakened to the reality of a weight on my back and shoulders. The weight of the thousand

"But Stephanie, this is not your cross to bear; this is not your burden to carry. That's why Jesus died."

bricks I carried became real. In that moment, I noticed how heavy my shoulders felt and how much my back ached. I felt raw. Ashamed. Aware of the worry. Aware of the lack of peace and hope.

The confrontation of pride inflamed my impatience. I wanted to run out of the coffee shop and scream, "Why does this have to be so hard!" But I couldn't move. My legs were weighed down beneath the emotional bricks.

"You're right. I let myself be buried under this heaviness, with worry and responsibilities that I shouldn't have lifted in the first place. I've been centered on my own ability. I don't have peace because I'm perpetually aware of my finite ability to make any impact or change in my brother's life. But I tried, darn it! I tried with all my might."

"That is heavy stuff," Kelly agreed. "I'm glad you can see that. You've put yourself through a lot."

I rummaged through my purse for a tissue, unable to see through my tears to find one.

"Do you think you can let it go?" she asked.

Wow, what a hard question. My whole body, mind, and spirit were on empty, tired and worn out. A life without peace couldn't continue.

"Do you think you have the courage to let God take care of him for you?" she asked.

My whole body, mind, and spirit were on empty, tired and worn out. A life without peace couldn't continue.

I continued to dig in my purse for a tissue, avoiding eye contact.

Did I have the courage?

"I don't want to feel the way I feel anymore," I admitted. "I want to be free of this burden, and from the lie that it's my job to save him. I don't know if I have the courage. But I want to let it go."

"Can I pray for you, Stephanie?"

"Sure, yes. Prayers are always welcome," I assured her, with a hoarse chuckle.

There, in the middle of the coffee shop, Kelly prayed over me.

"Lord, tonight I approach Your throne alongside my dear friend Stephanie. Lord, You know Steph's desire, and her heartache. You know how she longs to see her brother freed from alcoholism. We thank You that she confessed tonight that she's tried to save him in her own strength, without You. We ask tonight, Lord, even in this moment, that You heal her heart and mind. Free her mind from the grief she carries. Free her from the burden of hopelessness and worry. I pray, Lord, that You replace each with Your love, peace, hope, joy, satisfaction, and promises. Free her from the lies she's believed. In Jesus's name, amen."

In that moment, Kelly helped me find the courage to believe I could be free from the burden of Luke's addiction that I'd chosen to carry on my shoulders. I had found freedom from my savior complex, set free from the lie that I was not entitled to peace until Luke chose sobriety and life found its way back to normal.

That night, I started to let it all go. And that night, God had again showed Himself faithful, this time through a caring friend.

There are still days when I battle to let God be God. But I know my weakness for what it is, and I am able to hand it back over to God with a greater willingness than before.

In our weakness, Christ is strong. Christ changes hearts. He changes minds. Christ redeems. Christ saves. He gives abundant life. He loves us, each of us, even when we try to take His job.

SEARCHLIGHT
CONFESSIONS

L IKE AN ASPIRING SHERLOCK HOLMES, I trailed hot on the case of the hidden whiskey bottles. I sneaked into Luke's office and car as often as I could. I would show up a few minutes late to meetings I knew our whole management team would be at so that no one would see me rifle through his stuff. And I felt justified. I found my proof.

Yep, Steph, you were right. Good job, Steph; you found it. It's not hidden from you. You tracked it down.

I patted myself on the back like I was some hero. I patted myself on the back for violating Luke's personal space. I hunted repeatedly through his bags and desk drawers in search of evidence of crimes, the clues in his case.

I wonder now what the point was of these escapades, to search exhaustively to find proof of what I already knew was going on. I never removed it to confront him; the evidence stayed, seemingly undisturbed, in its respective hiding place. Maybe it fueled an adrenaline rush bred from manipulation and control. I now had evidence to hold over his head, should I need it. How vindictive it all was.

My actions as detective crossed some significant boundaries and broke trust. Such pursuit could only harm our relationship.

One afternoon, on my usual evidence hunt, I got caught red-handed. I was late for a management meeting when my husband walked by Luke's office and saw me hunkered down behind his desk, digging through his desk drawers.

"Uh, Stephanie . . . What are you doing?"

"Oh, hey, um . . . I just came to look for some samples I gave to Luke for a QC check that I need back to process."

Marshall, who knows me better than anyone, saw right through me.

"Stephanie, you've really got to stop this. This isn't right. What do you expect to find? And what good's it going to do if you find something?"

I stayed hunkered down, the desk a protective shield between us.

"It's only going to cause a wedge in your relationship," he persisted. "Aren't you supposed to be in a meeting, anyway?"

Perhaps the need to know where he hid his bottles, what he drank and how much, gave me a sense of control. When I'd find a bottle of alcohol, it put me in a position of power over him. The knowledge of his secrets presented the ability to manipulate him because I knew what no one else did—I knew his secrets and had the power to hold them over his head. And even he didn't know I knew his secrets. It made me feel powerful, and I craved that sense of power because I felt out of control.

With Morgan no longer in the picture, my feeling responsible to keep an eye on him grew even more unhealthy. I transitioned from detective to prosecutor, and both roles turned me into a lunatic. I began to imagine bottles that weren't there, made him guilty and put him on trial for deeds done even in innocence. I got more and more suspicious the more I searched, determined to catch him yet again.

My constant quest to discover his secrets led me to ask pointed questions—the passive-aggressive kind where you want the other person to know that you already know the answer. I never came right out and said, "I searched through your bags and found . . ." Of course not. That would have made me out to be sneaky, just as he was being when he hid it all. No, instead, I'd say, "I was looking for those samples I gave you. I thought maybe you'd put them in your work bag, but they weren't there. Do you know where I can find them?"

I sought to push him into a corner, convinced that his fear of being found out would force him to change his habitual patterns. I used the power of knowledge to make him feel weak. When Adam and Eve ate the forbidden fruit from the Tree of Knowledge of good and evil, it was the power and knowledge that attracted them, not the fruit itself.

I used the power of knowledge to make him feel weak.

I thought that in discovering his secret stashes, I gained god-like power. Instead, all I gained was separation. Just as God separated Adam and Eve from Himself and the garden when they ate of the fruit, I separated myself further and further from Luke the more I dug into his personal space without an invitation to do so.

A series of get-a-grip conversations with Marshall helped me see that the choices I was making and my actions were causing more harm than good. Somehow, I thought there would be fewer lies as the truth was uncovered. But lies begat more lies, not only Luke's lies to cover up his behavior but to explain away the evidence found. We grew further and further apart until, inevitably, he lost all faith and trust in me.

Why should he trust me? I violated his space. I violated his trust. And I crossed that line not once but multiple times. I didn't intend to damage our relationship. My actions and reactions did not align with my desire to be a shoulder for him to lean on. Sometimes it takes time for our hands, head, and feet to catch up to the heart.

I talk about prayer a lot throughout this book, but it is the single act that has never failed me. Prayer, a conversation with God, opened these eyes to a new perspective.

Maybe you've heard it said that prayer changes things. This is what I know to be true: Prayer changes me. Through prayer, whether sporadic or consistent, God changed my heart from a heart of condemnation to a heart of love. Why is that important? Prayer made it possible for me to improve my relationship with Luke, to forgive and be forgiven.

This is what I know to be true: Prayer changes me.

Prayer affected my need to know precisely every bottle's location and what he drank, how often, and how much. Through prayer, I lost the need to know, and the desire to be his cheerleader took over. Prayer changed my insistence on having power over him and power over the situation. Instead of lording the power over his head, I wanted him to trust that I was on his side, that I was there for him, no matter what. From here, trust could grow and be reestablished. Once, a need existed for lies and deception in order to hide from the condemnation. But now that we had freedom, lies were not required but honesty was, as good—or as bad—as it was.

We are each of us works in progress, always under construction. God used my husband to sharpen me over time, to help me consider the detriment of my detective behavior. Through this sharpening and prayer, I love better, and I do my best not to condemn, search, or seek power over another.

Power isn't something I need or that's beneficial for me to possess. Once I have it, old behavior patterns pull me in. I become, again, judge and juror. I dust off and don my old detective cap.

When I reach Heaven, that detective cap will be willingly left behind. But for now, I do my best to keep it under lock and key and pray for the urgency and desire to love well.

EMPTY EYES,
HOLLOW HEART

Y EARS OF THE STRESS of life's circumstances wore me down and beat me into submission. I lost the joyful and carefree girl I had once been. This new girl's forehead bore the signs of a permanent grimace, as if she had fought constant pain for years. Her mouth seemed to curl only downward, and her smile became merely a lesser frown. A stranger, constant in her distress. Looking in a mirror, I was face to face, eye to eye, with a woman whom I could not recognize, but the familiarity of her grief saddened me.

"Who are you? I don't even recognize you anymore," I said to my reflection.

She stared back at me with empty eyes.

... her smile became merely a lesser frown.

Why do you act this way? Why are you so angry with everyone? What did you do with the girl I used to know? You took her; you stole her away. You robbed her of so much goodness. All I'm left with is you.

The scowl lines in her forehead deepened.

What makes you think you have the right to change me?

Overwhelmed by her harsh stare, I walked away from the mirror.

When I took on all these added responsibilities and set myself up against an unattainable bar for success, I walked the path toward failure. I believed my heart could handle it. I tried to pave the way, like a bushman wielding a machete, whacking away everything that stood in the way for Luke to achieve sobriety.

I wanted Luke to beat addiction so badly that I could feel the victory—well, at least at that stage. I made it a habit to tell him, "I will never give up on you," which meant, "I will do whatever I can to make sure you never give up on you, and that you're successful, in spite of you."

How naive to think that I could stop someone else's addiction. But desperation had set in. God hadn't "fixed" Luke as quickly as I'd wanted Him to. In my mind, His slow response granted me the mission of front-line defense, air-traffic control, and cleanup crew.

Most of us do not willingly act out of an emotion that we know is inherently wrong. We act out of an emotion that we believe to be right, if only to find out later that our emotion lied to us and our emotion deceived us into action. The emotion clouded our judgment and led us to act in a way incongruent with our role in the circumstance.

After months—years—of life in the fog, I realized that what I felt toward the girl, the one who stared back at me from the mirror, was dislike. She couldn't stay.

The decision to shed her as my reflection required me to raise the white flag as if to say that addiction had won, that I could fight it no longer. Not an easy task. My pride and I met head on with this transformed image.

I knew that to come up for air and set forth on a new path meant I needed to face my failures as a mom and as a wife. But even that was a struggle.

I walked into the living room and stopped in my tracks. Turning toward the kitchen, where my daughter had disappeared just moments before, I shouted, "Cora Naomi, you get back in this room right this minute and pick up this popcorn you spilled everywhere. I can't believe you! You're six, after all! Have Dad and I taught you nothing? We pay all kinds of money for you to go to a great school, and you don't even have the courtesy to pick up after yourself." I was livid as I surveyed the mess in front of me.

Cora appeared in the doorway, confused. Tears flooded her gentle hazel eyes.

"But, Mama, I didn't knock it over. I only just came downstairs. I was in my room."

But intent on deflating all the tension that had built up inside me, I continued to yell at her.

"Whoa, what's going on?" Marshall said, as he walked into the house.

"What's going on? Your daughter made a mess and lied to me about it," I shouted. "Maybe you should deal with it since she gets that gene from you."

"Stephanie," Marshall said in his ever-calm voice that always inflamed me further, "it was Lydia who knocked the popcorn over. I told her I would help her clean it up, but I wanted to start the sprinkler in the backyard first. I'm happy to help clean it up."

I wish I could say that a bolt of lightning struck me that day and changed my heart. I wish I could say that I ran to my daughter, hugged her, and asked for forgiveness, but I didn't. Instead, I went berserk, "nuttier than a fruitcake," as my grandma would have said. My blood pressure spiked and I edged close to the cliff, falsely accusing her and lashing out at her for a simple spill. This is what life had become like for the woman in the mirror.

God has used my reflection on these times for me to point to my need for forgiveness, but also how necessary it is to forgive others. Children are a gift. They teach us about God's heart for people. They love with abandon. They love with openness and give many chances.

A couple of days passed before my pride subsided and I could recognize that my sorrow was not my children's burden to bear. I needed to apologize to Cora.

"Cora, sweetheart, Mommy needs to talk to you. I'm sorry for yelling at you about the popcorn. And I'm sorry that I accused you."

"What does 'accuse' mean, Mommy?"

"It means that I blamed you for doing something. And it was something you didn't even do. I did it without finding out first. In my mind you'd done it, when Lydia spilled the popcorn. Does that make sense, sweetie?"

"Yes, Mommy. And it's okay. I forgive you."

She hugged me. My heart swelled at her effortless forgiveness, her natural generosity, and I hugged her back, hard.

"What's wrong, Mommy? Are you okay?"

"Yes, darling, I'm fine. You just make me so happy. You're such a delightful little girl, and I love you so much."

"I love you, too, Mommy."

ↄ

MATTHEW, IN VERSE 12:34 (NKJV), writes, "For out of the abundance of the heart the mouth speaks." Despair had grown in abundance within me. Copious grief. Defeat. My heart was plagued with conflict. Yes, the woman in the mirror needed to leave. Her overwhelming sadness was no longer welcomed by the woman on my side of the mirror. But Jesus persisted in His pursuit of my life. He longed to permeate my life with His abundance and replace my despair with His limitless love.

LIABILITIES

I PICKED UP THE RECEIVER to make yet another sales call and forced myself to smile. (It's well-known that customers can "hear" you smile through the phone, and it's important to always talk to customers with a smile.)

As I listened to the phone ring, I heard the office's main door open and a low voice address the receptionist, but I couldn't hear the words over the whirring of the overhead vent. The phone clicked and a recording played in my ear.

"Hello, you've reached Tom and Cindy's Florals. We're sorry we can't come to the phone right now . . ."

Seriously? Oh, come on! How's anyone supposed to get orders from a voicemail? Maybe one of these days sales will be automated, and then I won't have to talk to anyone either.

In frustration, I rested my head on my desk.

Okay, Steph, let's refocus here. You can do this.

I picked up my head and was startled to see Luke in the doorway. Our paths crossed all too infrequently in the years that had followed the sale of our family business. Luke had stayed on to work with the new owners while I assumed the role of president of another business my parents owned.

"Hey, this is a surprise!" I said, as I got to my feet and came around my desk. "Great to see you!" As I approached, the familiar smell of alcohol filled my nostrils. Crestfallen, I embraced him tightly and strove to conceal the frustration I felt.

Does he know that I know? Should I say something? You're always the confronter, Stephanie. Must you always stir up trouble?

I wanted to shake his shoulders and yell at him.

Why can't you just give it up? Why do you want to kill yourself? AHHHH! So frustrating!

I could've screamed. But, instead, this time I chose silence, to hold all the questions inside.

We made small talk, though nothing seemed appropriate to talk about when this giant elephant filled the room.

Let it go, Stephanie!

I grew tired of the conflict-erupter role. Instead, I stiffled the urge and willed myself to carry on a plastic conversation full of ingenuous charm. To my mind, that seemed the best option.

> *I grew tired of the conflict-erupter role. Instead, I stiffled the urge and willed myself to carry on a plastic conversation full of ingenuous charm.*

"Pull up a chair," I invited, and sat behind my desk, which only served to highlight the difference in the power wielded.

"So, how's work for you?" I asked.

"It's okay. Not the same, you know? So much turnover. All the old guys, the ones with all the knowledge, either got fired or left."

"Yeah, I heard. That's a big gap for production."

Work had turned friendless for him, leaving him nostalgic for the good old days when we'd all worked together. My parents were now retired, Marshall worked for another company, and I had left to run this one. What we once knew as a comfortable yet challenging, dynamic family business was now owned by private equity managers. We each mourned the sale of the business. For Luke, it seemed a longer and harder process than mine—but then, he still worked there.

As he talked, a part of me glazed over, numb as I steeled myself to hear the same story I'd heard countless times before.

"I would like to make a move, Steph. Things are going south over there, especially for the salesmen. The incentives to sell are gone. They even told us not to sell because the machines are full. How do you tell a salesman not to sell?"

We sat there, steeped in the unspoken truth as to why he hadn't left. How could he begin at a new place—somewhere with new rules, new expectations, a new set of circumstances, new bosses to impress—when the drink carried more importance than work? More importance than his success? But how could I say that?

I couldn't.

There was a pause.

"Do you think," he finally said, "that sometime in the future, there could be a spot for me here to work with you?"

I knew how hard it must be for him to ask that, to ask his baby sister for a job. From where he sat, I appeared to have landed on my feet. I had it all together.

How can you ask that? Don't you realize I'm here, in this position, because I felt the pressure to cover up for you? I can't cover for you anymore. It's not within me to carry that burden. How is it possible to take on the responsibility to manage you? I can't even trust you!

I had to be straightforward. "It'd be nice if we could add you to the team, really. But, Luke, look at you. How could I trust you to get your work done? To learn our processes? To learn our product? And care for our customers? I'm really sorry, Luke, but I don't see you in any shape to work for me." My pity turned to irritation. "You would be nothing but a liability to me."

His eyes widened.

"I would be in constant worry that you got in a wreck," I continued. "I couldn't even consider such a thing until you got your life in order and stopped drinking."

The whir of the overhead vent was the only sound to disturb the silence that lingered between us.

"You do understand, don't you? You can see how it makes sense from this seat, right?"

You would be nothing but a liability to me.

He cleared his throat. "Sure. Yeah, I get it."

I rose and made my way around the desk. He stood and we gave each other a limp hug. The air hung thick around us.

I watched as he left, feeling unsettled yet determined to justify my response.

How could he? How does he even have the gall to ask me for a job? He has no idea what it's like to work weighed down with the persistent worry he requires. How could he come and ask me for help now? Doesn't he know I tried to get away from all his drama, from the worry, to not have to face it every day? After all, I have a reputation to think about. What would my employees think?

Of course it wouldn't work. Of course he couldn't work here.

﹏

SEVERAL MONTHS PASSED after that encounter, and in that period my relationship and time spent with God showed gradual improvement. I met with Him with greater frequency, and the desire to know Him, His will, and His heart grew.

During a commute home from work, God met with me in a powerful way. I heard with clarity His thoughts about the conversation I'd had with Luke. I heard my own words and cringed, feeling ill.

You would be nothing but a liability to me.

Did I really tell my own flesh and blood that a relationship with him was too great a risk? My body turned hot and queasy. My hands dampened with sweat.

God's voice followed the replay of my words, His gentle and clear words a rebuke.

You pray for Me to be gracious to your brother, but you do not extend to him the same grace that you expect from Me.

My pride had gotten the best of me. The time had come for humility.

I pulled over, reached for my cell phone and, tears streaming, dialed Luke. When he answered, I said, "Hey, how's it going?" Before he could get a word out, I added, "I need to apologize to you."

"What?" The confusion in his voice was apparent.

Out tumbled the story of how I had wronged him with words.

"I can't believe what I said to you. I'm sorry I said you were a liability. I'm sorry I was so harsh and insensitive." I took a deep, ragged breath. "God spoke to me about my words. He showed me how wrong I was. You are *not* a liability. No excuses for it," I added. "I'm sorry."

Luke's voice was soft, insistent.

"Steph, you don't need to apologize. I've been irresponsible. If anything, you showed honesty. I'm the one who has so much to apologize for. I've put you and Mom and Dad through a lot."

Tears coursed down my cheeks.

"I want you to know how deep my love is for you," I choked, "even though I don't show it very well sometimes. My heart's wrecked because I hurt you. Can you please forgive me?"

"Of course I forgive you," he said without hesitation, and I felt the weight of a thousand tons lift from me.

"Thank you," I breathed. "Thank you for your forgiveness. You didn't have to, and I wouldn't blame you if you never wanted to talk to me again."

We said our goodbyes, and I wove the car back into traffic, hitting stoplight after stoplight. It was one of my longest rides home.

Perhaps God knew I needed time to decompress and praise Him for the forgiveness I had received. I praised God that day because He had showed me the dark place in my heart.

I don't ever want to go back there.

Protect me, Lord, from a hard heart. Forgive me when I don't love my own flesh and blood or neighbor as myself.

As believers, we can adopt a mindset where we exist in a one-and-done kind of forgiveness. We forget what freedom feels like, the freedom that washed over us on the day we accepted Christ as our Savior, and all our sins were washed away.

Our forgiveness is a continual process, not static. Salvation does not make us perfect; it covers us with His blood. Salvation reestablishes our relationship with Christ. The old self is made new. I did not deserve the forgiveness that my brother extended to me that day. I had not earned it. It was his gift to me.

I will never again take for granted the power of "I forgive you," the power of "I am sorry."

> *Salvation does not make us perfect; it covers us with His blood.*

These are words that build up. How joyous to receive the words, "I forgive you." I believe it is built into our DNA to forgive and be forgiven. It has always been a part of God's plan for us.

PART 2
FROM FEAR'S GRIP

HOPELESS CAVERN

OVER THE YEARS, there've been seasons fraught with utter hopelessness. For a long time, it felt normal. The trenches of this fight, they are lonely. Crassness became my chosen self-preservation mode.

"Every word out of your mouth is negative, Stephanie."

I stared at my husband. "Excuse me? Every word? Come on, even if that's true, I have every right to be negative. The harder I try to help Luke, the farther he falls away. I can't win."

> *The trenches of this fight, they are lonely.*

I couldn't understand why Marshall didn't experience the same hopelessness. The negativity stemmed from despair over no action steps taken toward recovery, at least from my vantage point.

Now, on the other side of the great cavern of hopelessness, I can see and understand. The walk through hopelessness taught me how to experience hope. Without tragedy, without hardship, hope is easy, effortless, to assume. Hope is easy when life hands us a bowl of cherries. I heard someone once say, "It may pass like a kidney stone, but this, too, shall pass." Pretty sound advice, I'd say.

The walk through the cavern of hopelessness offered a choice: face the reality of what went on,

> *The walk through hopelessness taught me how to experience hope.*

live in a meaningful way, despite the hardship, or choose to hide out in the caves. Throughout many years of my life, cocooned in the darkness of my sorrow, I let circumstances triumph over me. I made that choice. No one could choose it for me. I used to pray, "I give my brother to You," yet go about my day with my focus on *What can I do to speed up this process? What can I do to help free my brother?*

As I walked through the cavern of hopelessness, hope became a laughable word because it seemed so far away from reality. The addiction became bigger than me, bigger than the family. It could not be solved with any amount of money, tools, templates, or self-help books. The addiction questioned my faith. And I hid in the caves, afraid to face the walk out of hopelessness.

My hopelessness was grounded in expectations, outcomes, and my timeline. Hopelessness ignored the truth of God. Therefore, in that cavern, I could not experience the fullness of hope that comes from Christ. His truth, based on His power, authority, and sovereignty, subbed for my own truth, one based on my capabilities, shortsightedness, and limitations.

Hope is born at the feet of Jesus. I knew I had to hand Luke over to Christ and ask Him to have His way—"Thy will be done on earth as it is in heaven," as Matthew tells us in verse 6:10 (KJV)—and not intervene, instead surrendering my will to God's will.

Hope is born at the feet of Jesus.

In a journal entry, I penned, "Lord, I want to be used by You, but I have decided not to act until Your Holy Spirit prompts me to do so. Lord, I trust that Your plans are better than mine. I believe that You work all things out for the good of those who love You. I believe that Your thoughts are higher than my thoughts, so even when I don't understand and can't see You or feel You move, I will still put faith and hope in You. I lay Luke at Your feet today. Help me, Lord, to leave him there; give me strength to not intervene. Give me strength to trust in Your plans. I give You my fear, hopelessness, and worry for this day. Guard my heart and mind so that I'm not tempted to be overcome by my circumstance. Help me, Lord, to rise above it, to have eyes to see You more clearly."

We cannot clench the problem *and* give it to God. Doesn't Isaiah say, in verse 56:8 (HCSB), "Is it not the will of the Father that He breaks chains, He sets the oppressed free, to untie the ropes of yokes too big for us to carry?"

He, too, wants recovery to come as swiftly as possible. My

belief and disbelief are locked in a dance, each eager to lead. God's protection is vital when I don't see answers as quickly as I'd like. I have learned to look for, seek out, and find God while I wait.

One of the quickest and surest ways to feel hopeless is to take on the role of savior. I believed my

We cannot clench the problem and give it to God.

brother's sobriety and recommitment to Christ fell within my ability to control. "What am I going to do?" became my mantra. Oh, the anger and frustration I harbored toward family—immediate as well as extended—because they, too, believed in Christ but seemed to me to sit idly by and not lift a finger to do anything to help fix him. Why didn't they try to help save him? Perhaps they didn't struggle with the same savior complex I did.

My strong desire to control Luke's choices and destiny caused me a lot of angst and guilt. I invited Luke to church and connected him with Christian male friends with whom he would have something in common. I hoped there would be a spark of friendship and someone else would help me with this load, to help pull all the responsibility I had shackled to my ankles.

I controlled and manipulated events and people to get him to "hear truth." I wore the mask of orchestrator and divine encounter creator. I devised plans that appeared, at least to me, to have been executed to perfection. All the stars aligned on many occasions.

Here, now, is a look at the hard honest truth. I am human. I am not, by any stretch of the imagination, divine. All my schemes proved that truth, perhaps too well. My plans—thoughtful. My plans—noble. But the delivery—well, it neared manipulative and cacophonous.

"Marshall, why don't you invite Luke to the ballgame with you, Chris, and Jud?"

"I guess I can. I was going to invite Josh—he's a big baseball fan—but I can invite Luke instead."

"That'd be wonderful if you'd do that for me—for him. Thank you!" I exclaimed, and pulled him in for a big kiss.

"Wait a minute," he said. "What schemes are you up to now?"

I looked up at him, innocently. "Li'l ole me? I'm not up to anything. I just thought it would be a great opportunity for Luke to meet some normal Christian guys, guys who share similar interests, guys who like to have a good time, too. Who knows?

Maybe they'll really hit it off and become friends. And it'd be you I'd have to thank," I added, beaming at him.

Full-blown mood swings, from drippy-sweet to heightened, uncontrolled emotions had hold of the steering wheel of my life. Over the years these interventions and schemes resulted in little evidence of success, in my terms. Today, I no longer hold tightly to my plans to wield the outcome desired for Luke. God granted freedom in my life as He taught me to let go of the hunger to get my way and gave me the courage to stop the control and dualistic behaviors, and to instead embrace freedom.

It took time.

This is not my job.

I told myself this truth over and over, stuck on repeat before it started to sink in. Repetition. Just like when I'd memorized the multiplication tables. Over and over. The same problems get the same answers. *It's not my job!*

It's not for me to even earn my own salvation. I am called to believe, to believe that God is who He says He is, and that He will do what He says He will do. And I believe that Jesus is His Son, who died on the cross for me.

Believe. Not one idea I have can be added to that. Not one action I do, or how I perform, will land me a seat in Heaven. Just believe. And I cannot believe for other people, as much as I want to. And what's more, I am not the Holy Spirit, capable of loosening and disentangling the blindfold of deceit.

I gained freedom to love Luke rather than save him. No amount of orchestration laid on him could help. I couldn't manipulate him into recovery. On God's path for me, I stopped the act of renegade follower and became a true follower of Christ, under His submission. With Christ at the helm, our relationship based in love, not expectation, could be rebuilt.

I gained freedom to love Luke rather than save him.

I close this chapter with one question: Are you ready to release the death grip of control and manipulation you have on your loved one's life?

Place the control in the hands of the rightful owner—back in the hands of your addict and of God. The control that you believe you have is a mirage. When the fog clears in your mind and heart, you'll wake up and see that the salvation you thought you could offer is just a fantasy.

CONDEMNED

J UMPING TO CONCLUSIONS is one of my spiritual gifts, one of my few areas of expertise. My brain is keen to hear the unspoken, to read body language, and to perceive the mood of everyone in the room. I experience each layer—moods, emotions, words, and physical cues—from others and take them on myself. Translation: I make assumptions based on how the cues and experiences compile in my mind. Sometimes—and only sometimes (*wink!*)—the conclusions I come to are wrong, or at least somewhat wrong.

When it came to my relationship with my brother, every encounter flooded me with the desire to fix versus understand. I sought for my opinion to be heard rather than to hear. More often than not, I heard what I wanted to hear and felt only what I wanted to feel. I found it difficult to initiate our conversations. Either we conversed superficially or I went in for the attack. Relationship in the in-between, somewhere between the surface and the depths of the heart, fell beyond my capability.

In all honesty, I feared he couldn't get better without my advice and help. But a relationship built on attacks is not a relationship; it's a prison. You find yourself locked up with poor expectations and misguided hopes.

> *A relationship built on attacks is not a relationship; it's a prison.*

Who wants a better relationship with someone who only criticizes and points out flaws? Not me. I wouldn't have wanted to be friends with myself, with that woman in the mirror, when such an awkward imbalance existed. The space between

The space between attack and the surface felt like a lie. It felt fake, as if nothing were awry.

attack and the surface felt like a lie. It felt fake, as if nothing were awry. I couldn't find balance or respond with a level head.

༄

"LUKE, PULL OVER," I said, my voice shaky yet firm.

The smell of alcohol permeated the car, yet I had chosen to ride with him anyway.

"What? Why? No. Why should I pull over?" he replied, clearly annoyed.

I mustered my best mom voice. "Pull over now."

Luke pulled into the parking lot of a rundown bowling alley.

"There," I said and pointed. "Pull over there, where those dumpsters are." He obeyed. "Now, give me everything you have," I demanded. "I want it all."

"What're you talking about? You're robbing me? Why are you acting like this?"

"You know what I'm talking about. Don't act innocent with me. I want every bottle of alcohol, open or not, that you've got hidden in this car. Open the trunk. I want to see what's back there."

Reluctantly, he pulled the release and I hopped out, feeling the prick of tears in my eyes as they swept the trunk. My hands shook with anger and disappointment. I collected every bottle and heaved them into the dumpster, feeling as fragile as the glass as it shattered. Luke stood and watched in miserable silence.

"One!" I counted.

Crash.

"Two!"

Crash.

"Three!"

Crash.

"Four!"

Crash.

We got back in the car. He rested his head on the steering wheel, tears streaming down his face.

In a hoarse voice, I whispered, "Father's Day, Luke—today is Father's Day. Couldn't you choose Dad and the family over alcohol even for one day?"

Proof of my emotional hangover, I let him drive me the rest of the way to lunch, the remainder of the drive carrying the stench of shame and defeat. He was cornered. Shamed. Indefensible.

Was it the right thing to do at that moment, to forcibly remove all of the alcohol from his car that day? It certainly proved ineffective, a forced degradation.

He hated me in those moments. I'm certain of it. It was undoubtedly the worst choice I could have made that day. Charged with emotion, I coerced him into humiliation. My words condemned him, conveying my complete disgust for his choices.

I could've said nothing other than kind and gracious words designed to build him up. I could've said, "I'm so glad you came to celebrate Father's Day with us, Luke. I'm so glad we could see you, hang out with you."

It took failure to see that no matter how many bottles I threw away, they would invariably reappear. The bottles were out of my control. My responses, words, and actions, however, were within my control. After several fails, I stopped throwing bottles away, to intervene, corner, and manipulate his emotions. Instead, I let it go.

Marshall, the constant, solid, logical voice of reason approached me about how I was handling— or not handling—my relationship with Luke. The anxiety within me sat like a rocket on a launcher, ready to explode at any moment. Marshall saw through the emotion and illogical behavior. He knew my heart.

"How would you feel about me," he asked, "if every time we saw each other I pointed out one of your flaws?"

"Could you find that many flaws in me?" I teased, trying to laugh off my discomfort.

"No, in seriousness, how would you feel? Consider also that my accusations were biased, based on a limited view of you."

I felt a flash of irritation, followed by realization.

"I'd be annoyed, and probably want to give you a swift kick to the groin," I admitted.

He nodded. "Yes, and those are valid reactions. But how would you *feel*? Think about it. Over months—years—of my doing that every single time you saw me, what would that do to your self-esteem?"

I looked at him, mortified.

"It would kill me. I'd be angry, sure, but, more than that, devastated that this person I love so much sees only my flaws." I took an uneven breath. "I'd be crushed."

The lens of contempt that filtered my view of Luke dissolved, thanks to the courage of my husband, who had responded to a prompt from God to talk to me about how I jumped to conclusions and showed no compassion or care for the carnage I left behind after my attacks. Before that, I'd convinced myself that Marshall simply didn't understand.

"What if your own brother faced these challenges?" I said, defensively. "You'd respond just as I have." Even as I said those words, I knew it wasn't even close to the truth. Marshall possessed the ability to be supportive and speak truth to people in ways that I could only dream of emulating. He speaks always to me as a patient teacher in this area, which I find extraordinary.

About a week went by before I was willing to let go of pride and ask God to intervene, my thoughts filled with Marshall's advice to communicate out of love, not anger, just as Marshall had done with me.

I prayed.

Heavenly Father, Creator, Sustainer, Giver of life and all good things. I know my words have not brought honor to Your name. I know I have fallen short in my ability and even in my desire to control my tongue. I also know that Your Word says that words cut like a knife, capable of life and death. I fear my words toward my brother have been most often words of condemnation and death, instead of words of hope, joy, and peace. Lord, I want my words to be seasoned with salt, able to heal the brokenhearted, to bind up their wounds. On my own, Lord, I will fail. But with Your help, this area of weakness for me will become strong because You are strong. May the words of my mouth and the meditations of my heart be glorifying to You, Lord God. In Jesus's name.

How different my relationships would be with family, friends, acquaintances, and even strangers, I thought, if words of life poured out of me instead of hateful words. It takes effort to build relationships, and it takes effort to heal the wounds of bitterness and anger that hurtful words have caused. Time, slowly and steadily, does heal.

By God's grace, the conversations between Luke and me no longer feel forced or vindictive. It took several years for me to stop anticipating how our conversations would go and dwelling on every word.

Our relationship is not where I would like it to be, not yet. We do not speak often. And when we do, superficial conversations are the norm. These days I talk less and leave quiet space for him to fill, and if he chooses not to, that's okay. I can live with the quiet space. I would rather contend with the quiet than speak words I'd regret.

Trust is a two-way street and is impossible to curate from condemnation. The fruit of trust is a healthy and strong relationship. It cannot grow in the shade behind the walls and barriers we set up for self-preservation. Each side must strive to display worthiness of trust while at the same time creating a safe atmosphere to bridge the gap of past broken trust.

> *Trust is impossible to curate from condemnation.*

Trust and undue conclusions cannot coexist. I'd tried to cultivate a relationship with Luke so he would trust me enough to listen to my so-called recommendations. But our relationship was doomed from the start because I tend to jump to conclusions. Once I abandoned that behavior, I had a chance to heal past hurts. Through slow, alleviative intentions, I keep trying, even today, to earn Luke's trust.

REMEDY FOR WHAT-IF

C HRISTIAN AUTHOR AND PREACHER Max Lucado writes, "Can you imagine a life with no fear? What if faith, not fear, was your default reaction to threats?" My initial response to that first question was once a resounding "No!" No, I couldn't imagine a life without fear, where fear was not my immediate reaction to my what-if questions. Most days, these dreadful thoughts tempted me to live out of my fear instead of living out of my faith. I allowed my mind to be held captive by these paralytic thoughts, and my trepidations produced a physical impact on my body.

Many times, all the what-ifs engulfed me in fear. Drowned me in disbelief. Drenched me in discouragement.

The negative speculations, over time, developed into incessant back pain and landed me on a

My trepidations produced a physical impact on my body.

chiropractor's table, receiving months of care. I had not suffered a fall or a car accident. I suffered a broken heart and mental torment that surfaced as back pain. By ten in the morning, my back ached, and each negative thought became a spear-like pain aimed straight into my spine.

My chiropractor would prove to be a faith counselor in disguise. My patient visits with Dr. Keen doubled as faith examinations, which siphoned the poison of the misguided truths I drank. My appointments forced me to reckon with whose truth I believed, mine or God's, a choice to harbor the "See? I told You so, God" attitude in my heart, or to trust God implicitly instead.

I asked myself: If this fear came true, then why wouldn't

My appointments forced me to reckon with whose truth I believed, mine or God's.

the other fears come true as well? I couldn't help but think that Luke was going to die, and that I couldn't help him.

I couldn't strain toward the past. I couldn't try to re-create an old reality, or find satisfaction or dissatisfaction, in our circumstances. I knew that I was neither ready nor able to face the reality of a deeper plunge alone. No more straining to un-know the news. I knew it; I couldn't un-know it. It existed, planted inside my memory. But just because the memory was seeded there didn't mean that the thought, the recollection of those moments, had to haunt me.

Alcoholism changed the fabric of our lives. When faced with the news of yet another relapse, I ran to the only place I could find comfort beyond all measure.

❧

"STEPH, I NEED YOUR HELP," Luke gasped. "I got in an accident and my car's in pretty bad shape. Do you think you could pick me up from the dealership? I need a ride back to my apartment."

"Oh no! Are you sure you're okay? Did anyone get hurt?" I couldn't keep myself from adding, "Were you drinking?"

"I'm fine, and no one else got hurt. I just slid on some ice and hit the embankment. It's pretty slick out this morning."

"Okay." I was relieved no one else was involved. "You'll have to wait on me to get to the dealership. I'm not dressed yet, and I have to take the girls to daycare and school."

That was a lie. I didn't believe he'd slid on the ice, and I didn't have to take the girls to school. But I needed a little time to hide out in my bedroom closet, which I had made a mini sanctuary for me, a haven to release all my fears, all the cries for help, and all the questions I wrestled with. I was grateful that he was safe but wrecked by the fact that my ever-lingering fear of the inevitable, an alcohol-fueled car accident, might have come true.

I didn't know for sure if Luke was drinking again, but my mind didn't hesitate to leap to that conclusion. In this closet, with its clothes and shoes, so much more was housed beyond material possessions. This closet held within it prayers, songs of praise, whimpers of a broken heart, and utterances of scripture.

That morning, a morning that had started out abysmally, God comforted me in my sanctuary, between those four walls. No, I didn't have answers for this relapse, but the need to have answers had vanished.

As I read and reread verse after verse, the words freed me from the desire to fix and control. The words from the Holy Book gathered the pieces of my broken heart and wove them back together, piece by piece, verse by verse.

Face down, despite our life in chaos, it was still and quiet in that closet. Only the murmur of my voice as I recited the scripture could be heard. God recalled His promises to me from His Word.

The words from the Holy Book gathered the pieces of my broken heart and wove them back together, piece by piece, verse by verse.

Romans 15:13 (ESV) says, "May the God of hope fill you with all joy and peace in believing, so that by the power of the Holy Spirit you may abound in hope," and I replied just as the father of the child had in Mark, verse 9:24b (ESV): "I believe; help my unbelief!"

As I read over verses I had written and rewritten in my journal, it felt as if God Himself were speaking these words straight to my heart. My anxious thoughts and worry faded into my surroundings. Strength and courage returned, and I felt I could walk out the door confident.

These verses became the healthy antidote for my sick mind, for the what-if poison that I consumed. These verses redirected my attention back to God. The promise in Lamentations 3:25–26 (TM) is that "God proves to be good to the man who passionately waits, to the woman who diligently seeks. It's a good thing to quietly hope, quietly hope for help from God. It's a good thing when you're young to stick it out through the hard times."

I left the house that morning faced with the reality of a what-if and learned that God upholds His end of the bargain. He is faithful in bringing peace.

I arrived at the dealership, and by God's power, my anger, anxious thoughts, and worry over another relapse were gone.

The moment I laid eyes on Luke, I knew he hadn't been drinking. I felt such relief, mingled with embarrassment that stemmed from my initial lack of faith. My what-if didn't win because I'd hidden myself in my closet to seek hope. I'd found hope and peace, and the realization that my worry over the what-if had been unfounded.

It was the juxtaposition of hopefulness in fear and heartache that brought me to my knees, weighed down by a burdened mind. While I was on my knees, God lifted from me the sorrow, defeat, trouble, and worry. He exchanged my burden for His yoke, which is easy and light. While I faced my own soul's depravity, God's Word alone, His virtue, His uprightness, provided me the courage to carry on, even as one of my fears had proved not to be what it could have been. I had made it through.

I didn't make it alone. I couldn't have made it without God's help.

> *Memorized scripture is the air that fills my floaties and keeps my head up and out of the waters of despair.*

I found a secret serum to combat negative thoughts. The secret is to chase the venomous thoughts away with a verse. The verses distract my mind, a scripture like Hebrews 12:2 (GW): "We must focus on Jesus, the source and the goal of our faith. He saw the joy ahead of Him, so He endured death on the cross and ignored the disgrace that it brought Him. Now He holds the honored position—the one next to God the Father on the heavenly throne."

Scripture memorization, for me, has become a spiritual life preserver. Memorized scripture is the air that fills my floaties and keeps my head up and out of the waters of despair. Verses banish destructive thoughts from my mind by supplanting them.

Replace the thoughts; do not ignore them. If they are left to fester and are not replaced, they become obsessions, and anxiety spirals out of control. My obsessive thoughts of slow progress stole much joy. I wanted to see Luke make healthy choices, to see him make decisions for his good, not his detriment.

God often asks me if I will continue to trust Him, even when I cannot see, even when there is no resolution, even when I do not understand His plans. I trust that He will work it out in bigger ways than I can comprehend.

If I could be obsessed by how much He loves me and cares for me instead of obsessing over that which I have no control, I would live lighter. He is worthy of our infatuation, a reason to find hope. In his book *The Miracle of Hope*, Charles L. Allen said, "On every page of the Bible there are words of God that give us reason to hope . . . In the promises of God I find inspiration and a new hope."

STAINS AND LABELS

As I washed my face before bed one evening, I heard a commercial for Tide laundry detergent, and was struck when a man's voice said, "All they see is the stain."

"Whoa," I thought. "That's heavy." Indeed, such philosophical truth from a detergent commercial. Once we notice a stain on someone, it's hard to not stare. That's the reality of the human condition in terms of external appearances. How much truer is it for personalities, life choices, and what side of the tracks we grew up on?

The stain was immediately visible to me and impossible to ignore when I looked at my brother, like the flash of a hazard light. I found it difficult to see beyond the stain of his addiction. I needed to look past the pasta sauce on his shirt and see the person inside.

But how?

It took a laundry detergent commercial to open my eyes to my shortsightedness. I saw the stain in front of me, zeroed in on its details, and lost sight of the big picture. I had a huge plank in my eye, while all along I had chosen to focus on and critique the sawdust I'd found in my brother's eye. My shortsighted tendencies crippled my ability to see him altogether, to see him as a person. While he faced addiction, in the earlier years I treated him like a problem to be dealt with instead of someone with a life-threatening disease. I reacted with a quick temper, angered, and as a recorder of his wrongs.

I needed to look past the pasta sauce on his shirt and see the person inside.

But when I look at him as a person, see the whole of who he is and was, not just the stain and not just a disease, that's when gentleness and compassion come. I don't get angry with him—with Satan, yes, but with him, no—and work instead on the plank in my eye.

For the longest time, I didn't stop and take time to ask Luke why. I wondered why he needed to use alcohol but was content to draw my own conclusions. I assumed it was his way to escape. It saddens me, the charades I pulled designed to help him get better, based only on my assumptions of the root cause.

～

I WANTED LUKE'S PERMISSION to write a book about how God had used his addiction to transform me from a narcissistic, erratic mental case to a humbler, Christ-focused woman. It was at this intersection of vulnerability and humility that I finally asked him why. I didn't know what he would say, whether he would tell me to shove it or embrace it.

"Luke, I want to share a story with you."

"Okay. I like a good story."

"One morning, in my quiet time before anyone else in the house was awake, I was doing my normal routine, reading from a devotional book and journaling. I came across this verse in Isaiah: 'The Lord God has given me the tongue of those who are instructed to know how to sustain the weary with a word.' As I read those words, I felt God speak to my heart and say, 'Write your story; tell others of how I have changed you. Speak. Write and speak.' So, I believe God has asked me to go to an uncomfortable place."

"What, like tell your story in a foreign country or something?" he teased.

"No," I laughed, "though it's not farfetched. No, it's closer to home than that." I took a deep breath. "When God spoke to me, He asked me to write. He asked me to share my testimony. But I need your blessing."

"But why do you need my approval? It's your story."

I hesitated. "It's actually *our* story. You see, God used your addiction to reach me, to change me. I knew all the 'Christian-ese' words, and I did the respectable behaviors as a regular church attender—morals and stuff, you know."

"Yeah?"

"But my heart was far from God. My heart and mind were not aligned to God's plan. I was critical and judge-y, and I thought I could save you myself," I said with an embarrassed smile. "How messed up is that?"

He grinned. "Yep, that's pretty insane."

"Anyway, he changed me from the inside out. I'm not the same person I was, even three years ago. He made me new."

Luke looked at me with raised eyebrows, as if waiting for the punch line.

"I need your blessing because this story, my story, doesn't exist without you. You and your journey are central to how God changed me."

He rubbed his hands together, thinking, and fidgeted with his water glass, inching it back and forth, before leaning back in his seat to meet my gaze.

Nodding, he said, "If our story can help save one life, it's worth it. If it can help ease the pain of a single family member, then yes. *Yes!* Write! I'm impressed by your courage in taking this on. If I can help in any way, let me know."

I exhaled audibly, unaware until then that I'd been holding my breath. What a gift from God. Even though the struggle continued, Luke didn't want others to face what we had faced, were still facing. It was time to ask.

"Luke, what first drew you to alcohol all those years ago? Were you trying to escape? To hide? To run?"

He took off his ball cap and scratched the top of his head. He looked down at the omelet before him, as if debating whether to share that intimate part of himself.

"Growing up," he said, "I never felt good enough. I always tried to measure up and always felt I missed the mark."

I nodded. This was something we shared.

"Having been around adults a lot, I communicated well with them. I could talk politics, music, sports, and cars when I was young, but I struggled to relate to people my own age." He paused and looked around the restaurant. I leaned in and laid my hand on top of his.

"Through high school," he continued, "I was self-conscious about relating to girls, and I guess I used alcohol to become the guy I wanted to be—uninhibited and funny. When I drank, I suddenly had the power to light up a room. Girls responded to me because I wasn't so uptight anymore. I was relaxed and free to be the real me, the one hidden inside."

I wondered how a person who embodied such brilliance and capability as he did could get so lost. The pressure to perform? He possessed talents and gifts, but relationships didn't come easily. I squeezed his hand.

"Thanks for sharing your heart with me."

I thought for a moment about all he'd said. "I understand the pressure to be someone different—taller, straighter hair, louder voice, funnier, smarter. We're taught to think whoever we are isn't good enough. Truth be known, it's only in the last year or so that I've felt content in my own skin. I'm finally at peace with who God made me to be."

"That is good news. I wasn't sure you'd understand." He chuckled. "Good news that you're comfortable with who you are, that is, not that you wouldn't understand. You know what I mean."

I smiled. "I do. I understand. God has taught me that the role He's given me is one that only I can play. He needs me to be me. I've fought with Him about it, because I felt the way He'd designed me wasn't good enough for what He was asking me to do. And maybe it's not. But that's the very reason I lean in to Him and trust His sufficiency. Where I lack, He fills in the gaps."

Why, I wondered, didn't I have the courage or wherewithal to ask Luke this years before?

We talked and talked that morning, and over omelets and coffee he revealed his heart to me. With it laid bare, the stain I'd fixated on began to fade.

He had wrestled all this time with his identity. He didn't know how much God loved him. He couldn't see God's plan or the purpose he would fill.

I was engaged in my own wrestling match with identity. Pride. Performance. Pleasing others. I was overwhelmed by relentless questions: "Am I good enough?" and "Is this good enough to meet someone's standards for me?" I did indeed get it.

My lips twitched. "We are more alike than you know, brother."

He had chosen a path that I just as easily could have chosen in my race to find my identity. By God's grace, I had chosen a different path. Yet I had found my identity in Christ. He said I was enough, that I was perfect, exactly how He made me.

The alcohol, as it wore off, reiterated the same old lie: You're not good enough. It was no wonder my words to Luke had fallen on deaf ears. He'd heard the lies of insufficiency too often. And I didn't invest enough time in our relationship to earn the right to know why he'd chosen alcohol, to know his heart and look past the stain.

How much deeper would my love for him have been had I taken time to understand his battle with identity? It's funny how once you *The alcohol, as it wore off, reiterated the same old lie: You're not good enough.* can see yourself in someone else, your whole perception of them changes. We want people to be gentle and understand us; it's harder to love when we don't take time to understand.

When I listened, I empathized because I heard his heart. I know the pain he felt, and the anxiety he bore—his hurt became real to me. Listening to his reasons helped me see Luke, not just a stain.

Zephaniah 3:17 (AMP) says, "The Lord your God is in your midst, A Warrior who saves. He will rejoice over you with joy; He will be quiet in His love (making no mention of your past sins), He will rejoice over you with shouts of joy."

God rejoices over us with shouts of joy even though He knows the depths of our depravity. He knows us better than we know ourselves and yet He loves us. Whether we are harlot or alcoholic, slanderer or thief, He loves us just the same.

FEARS RELEASED

M Y YOUNGER DAUGHTER, Lydia, loves to shop and is quite
chatty, but she also loves to hide in the clothing racks, which
has caused me to panic any number of times. One afternoon
around the holidays, we were shopping at a busy department
store filled with lots of shoppers sifting through the racks. The
excitement of Christmas filled the air. Lydia and I chatted as we
shopped for gifts for our family members.

I looked around. No sign of Lydia. I scanned the racks. She
was nowhere to be seen in the crowded store.

"Lydia, oh Lydia, come out, come out wherever you are!" I
sang, feeling slightly apprehensive.

No response.

"Lydia," I called, "come out, come out! It's time to move on
to another store."

I squatted down to peer beneath the clothes racks, hoping to
find her balled up, giggling, as she hid from me. I looked left
and right, beyond and behind me. I didn't see her anywhere. No
little legs dangled under any of the racks. Anxiety bloomed and
my heart pumped adrenaline through my body, faster and faster.

I raised my voice in my more serious "mom tone," trying not
to sound anxious.

"Lydia, Ly–di–a. Where are you, sweetie? Lydia!"

After what felt like an eternity, I heard a giggle coming from
the fitting rooms. I squatted down again to peek under the stall
door and saw two little legs. At that moment, her sweet face popped
under the door, pigtails dangling. She was grinning from ear to ear.

"Wasn't that a great hiding place, Mommy?"

"Oh, my word, Lydia, you scared me half to death. I thought I'd lost you. Honey, you can't run off like that. Mommy couldn't bear it if anything happened to you."

Her face fell. "I'm sorry, Mommy." But then she giggled again. "But it was a good spot, wasn't it?"

"It certainly was," I said, unable to keep from smiling at her glee. "Just don't make it a habit to hide in the fitting room!"

The difference between the fear of losing sight of a child in a public place and when you grapple with addiction is that it comes to an end when the child is found. With Luke, for years I couldn't rest, couldn't escape the fear that I carried. I couldn't take a single peaceful deep breath. I became more acquainted with fear in my lifetime than I care to admit or even think about.

Fear owned me, like a captive. Life, death, potential harm, consequences, health concerns, relationships lost, left as an only child, parents' health, reputations, and my own health. Fears: Am I good enough, strong enough, stable enough, titled enough, positioned well enough, worth enough, smart enough, credentialed enough to make an impact here?

After most blowups, I'd think: *How did I get here?* Frightened that the horrible thoughts that permeated my brain could or would prove real, these fears, left uncounseled, tore me apart from the inside out. I didn't have the answer. Blinded by the darkness, I couldn't see how to escape my panic-stricken life. I needed to reach a place where I could breathe in His peace and exhale all the fear that consumed me.

One night about a year and a half ago, I attended a Bethel Worship Nights concert with several girlfriends. While there, my fears were laid bare before God. They couldn't be stuffed deep down inside anymore. I'd become expert at hiding them, but that night they poured out of me as I entered worship, postured to praise God. Song after song, the layers of fears cracked and broke loose.

Tears of surrender flowed down my cheeks as I breathed in His peace through the song, "No Longer Slaves." The worship leaders sang out, "You split the sea, so I could walk right through it. My fears are drowned in perfect love. You rescued me, so I can stand and sing. I am a child of God."

The house lights were off, bathing the audience in total darkness. The only lights emanated from the stage, drawing our focus toward Christ. Thousands were in attendance, but my encounter with Jesus was as if His attention was focused solely on me, and I fixed my sights on Him alone. The song lyrics echoed between my heart and His. As those words were sung, I sang aloud, too, and my heart broke open in response.

"I'm no longer a slave to fear. I am a child of God." I sang at the top of my voice, with all I had within me.

My hands raised high, songs poured forth from my soul, open to all He prepared for me to receive. God ripped away the fears that plagued my spirit and blanketed them with His love.

When the concert ended, I turned to my friends.

"Wow! I don't want to leave. Does it have to be over?"

"I know, right?" Kari agreed. "I walked in this auditorium feeling so heavy. I've been so anxious of late, but I feel so light now."

"I know what you mean!" Abbe said. "I felt like God and I were just hanging out, just me and Him, for two hours. Incredible! He really did a work in my heart tonight."

The concert provided a worshipful space to encounter God in a fresh way. He chiseled away at each fear. And to be there surrounded by my dearest friends enhanced the experience. Each of my friends had come to the concert that night burdened by family issues, financial stress, job stress, anxiety, and fear, and God had freed each of us that night. Not that the problems went away, but He freed us from the fear, anxiety, depression, and hopelessness that surrounded the problems. We walked out lighter than when we'd walked in.

I prayed out of a thankful heart the whole ride home: "Lord, thank You for not leaving me stuck in my fears. Father, You know I don't want to live like that. I want to be usable for You, and now I can be."

Each of us can be liberated from the bondage of fear. When we know who we are at the deepest core of our being, Whom we belong to, Who has the final say, and that He is on our side, how can we be a slave to fear? God is a liberator—a liberator from fear, anxiety, depression, and all that trips us up and keeps us from living in abundance.

I am not a slave anymore to my thoughts and fears. They no longer control me. Galatians 4:7 (NKJV) says, "Therefore you are no longer a slave, but a son; and if a son then also an heir through Christ." I am an heir of God through Christ. I am His child. I belong to Him. He is my Abba.

PART 3
TO FAITH'S SUMMIT

BOUNDARY LINES LAID

THERE IS A FINE LINE between meeting a need for a loved one and enabling irresponsible behavior. Crossed boundary lines are often described as codependency. What does it look like to have a codependent or boundary-crossed relationship? In short, it is downright unhealthy.

Boundaries are not to restrict access between people or build up walls. Henry Cloud and John Townsend, in their book *Boundaries*, say it is about the recognition of ownership—who owns what—so that communication can be open and how we relate to others can be crystal clear and defined. They challenge us to ask the question, "Where does my property end and theirs begin?"

Cloud and Townsend ask these questions in the *Boundaries Participant's Guide*: "What is the difference between responsibility *for* another person and responsibility *to* another person? Which is healthy? Why?"

I pondered this question, and many more, with the women's Bible study that I attended at church, which included five women from five generations. It offered a beautiful and dynamic picture of "iron sharpening iron." The older women in the group poured themselves into and encouraged the younger generations. Yet the older ones also learned from the younger generations involved. Balanced and supportive. I drew so much strength and wisdom from them as we worked through the authors' challenges.

"In which pattern, or patterns, can you see yourself, Stephanie?" asked Caryn, the group facilitator.

"Hmm," I said, studying my doodles on the page in the workbook, knowing full well what the answer was. "I guess the best fit in terms of a pattern for my life would be 'Controllers hear "no" as simply a challenge to change the other person's mind. Controllers can't respect other people's limits.'"

Controllers can't respect other people's limits.

The women all smiled knowingly at me, with love in their eyes.

"Thanks for sharing, Stephanie. I know it can be hard to admit to and verbalize an area in which we struggle, but you're surrounded by women who are right with you," Caryn assured me and looked around at the group. "Would anyone else like to share the behavior pattern trap they fall into?"

Rochelle spoke up and I leaned in. She faced vulnerability head on, like no one I had ever met before.

"I think I'm a mixture of these behaviors. I'm compliant—I need to learn how to tell people 'no'—and I'm also avoidant in that I don't ask other people for help. I want to fix everything for everyone else, but I resist having anyone help me. It's not that I don't want the help; it's that I don't always feel worthy of the help. So I avoid the situation and people, and I miss out on a lot of support."

"I'm also a combination," Mary admitted. "I'm a controller and avoidant. It seems I've put up so many boundaries in my own life to self-protect due to a lot of trauma I faced as a child and even in my young married years—barriers to keep people out and to try to control everyone else. It takes a lot of work, a lot of effort, to maintain those walls and keep everyone out, and still seek to control. Whew, makes me tired just thinking about it!"

"I see myself as a combination as well," Rachel said. "Is it possible to be all three: controller, avoider, and compliant?"

We chuckled. We all felt the same way. It felt good to have a safe place to admit tendencies like these and work on them—not excuse them but really work on them. Our awareness of these typical boundary-related behavior patterns was the launch pad, the starting point to improve our relationships.

Relationships with substance abusers fall into a vicious cycle where boundary lines are marked and then re-marked, over and over. More harm than good comes from the repeated boundary shifts and lack of consistency. Trouble comes as our feet cross over into their property, into the areas they're responsible for.

We take claim over what isn't ours because we convince ourselves we are better property managers. Outside of the fence line, beyond the property lines—that terrain is not ours, it's not our concern. It's not our job to fix, or manage, or repair. The heart's desire is to fix and make things better, no matter what it costs us. But in the end, it just doesn't work. We need to stay inside the boundary lines; our own property management is difficult enough.

Eying the rearview mirror, there is so much that I wish I could go back and change. The greatest gift and blessing now is time. I have time to make amends and live the days ahead better than I lived the days behind me.

> *We take claim over what isn't ours because we convince ourselves we are better property managers.*

I suffocated God out of this situation, despite my having always beckoned Him to intervene. I was of two minds: I wanted God to take over, but I was too afraid of the outcome if He did, so I would step in. And I was too afraid of the outcome if I allowed Luke to fall, if I relinquished to him responsibility for his own well-being. It seemed smarter, or more reasonable, for someone supposedly more in their right mind to be in control. Yet now I see that my so-called right mind was colored by a misguided perspective. My mantra was, "You're in good hands with Stephanie," not unlike the car insurance commercial. And I bought into it hook, line, and sinker.

> *My mantra was, "You're in good hands with Stephanie," not unlike the car insurance commercial.*

I allowed an intoxicated Luke to be around my kids and play Barbies with them. My attachment to action said these decisions were permissible because, at the very least, if Luke was in my home where I could keep an eye on him, I knew he wouldn't be in trouble. Instead of helping, however, what I had done was take responsibility away from Luke.

The time had come to establish some boundaries and have hard conversations. My stomach still gets all tied up in knots when I think about the hard conversation we had and the boundary I established: "You won't be around me or my girls when you've been drinking."

It seemed harsh, but my daughters' safety and well-being had to come first. My focus on being the commander of my brother's life ended, and responsibility was returned to its rightful owner, while I focused on my roles as wife and mother.

How do you say with eloquence, "I've seen the worst of you, and despite that I still love you—but I can't help you anymore"? It sounds so hurtful and harsh. But it had to be said.

This was one of the hardest conversations I'd had with anyone. The day arrived to let go of the control—to know I'd caused harm and to now let it go, to know I should step aside and let the chips fall where they may.

"I've seen the worst of you, and despite that I still love you—but I can't help you anymore."

I met Luke for lunch on a workday, and of course the best place to deliver bad news to someone is in a public place, like a restaurant. I could have picked a better place perhaps, but I knew it would be a quiet place to talk.

Over sushi and hot tea, I said, "I want you to be around my family. My girls need to have an uncle close, and you're it. You know how much Uncle Mark meant to us growing up. The girls have that same love for you."

He traced his chopsticks through the soy sauce on his plate, as if drawing a symbol of his thoughts for me to interpret.

"I know, Steph. I love your girls—they're funny and sweet, and I enjoy being around them."

"That's why it breaks my heart to tell you that Marshall and I have decided you can't be around our girls if you're drunk. They're getting older, and they'll notice. And when they ask me questions about your behavior or why they can't see you, I'll tell them they have to ask you."

"Steph, I get it. I know I'm not the greatest role model."

"One more thing, Luke. No more late-night phone calls, and I can't help you anymore with your car, your apartment, your girlfriends, whatever. We can't help you. You have to help you. God can help you, and He will, if you ask Him to."

I took a drink of my now tepid tea and felt a rush of nausea as remorse surged through me, causing me to question everything

I'd said. Was I making the best choice for my family? I'd hurt him again.

This is not your battle, Stephanie. Stay the course.

I put my elbows on the table and rested my forehead in my hands.

"I'm sorry it has to be this way, but it's what's best for my family. They're my priority now."

Luke sat there, staring at his plate, expressionless. He looked pale and aged.

What is going through his mind, I wondered. *Does he hate me? Will my girls ever have the chance to know him as I knew him?*

With the boundary lines now laid, I said, "We love to be around you. You make us laugh. I feel, though, as if I have robbed you of responsibility. Maybe things would have turned out differently, or better, if I had not intervened as often."

He said nothing, just continued to stare at his plate for the rest of the meal, never letting his eyes meet mine. That was the hardest part. I couldn't see his eyes. I couldn't see how what I had said landed for him.

After that conversation, Luke experienced some scary days and, as usual, the temptation to jump in and help was strong.

I thought about what I'd tell my kids when they chewed on their fingernails: "If you can't stop biting your nails, sit on your hands, or I'll sit on your hands for you."

"If you can't stop biting your nails, sit on your hands."

I practiced what I preached and sat on my hands as temptation drew me to run to Luke's rescue.

IN GOOD HANDS

W<small>E ALL WANT THE ASSURANCE</small> of safety, insurance for our valuables, to guard against loss. Our lives, our health, our homes, our cars and boats—you name it—can all be insured. Even our pets. As family members of someone who struggles with addiction—any form of addiction—we are often passionate and want to be that insurance, that safety net for our loved ones. We want our hands on the situation. The desire to be front and center, to get to the bottom of it, seems logical.

Hands off and hands out is really the best policy.

What?

I know. It's harder than hard. Heart strings in a constant tug of war. No one wants to see a child, parent, husband, or wife hurting. We want to do anything within our power to stop the hurt.

Yet what if breakthrough rests more in what *isn't* done than in what *is* done? What if the ability not to intervene is more impactful than any help we might offer? It seems counterintuitive, even unkind; however, this position, this state of mind, allows God the opportunity to display His power. And as His power is displayed, our faith builds.

> *What if breakthrough rests more in what* isn't *done than in what* is *done?*

God is hands-on, and we are hands-off. He knows what's best. God is glorified when we display trust in Him. He is pleased when we get out of the way and let Him place His healing hands on the situation.

Trouble comes via the satisfaction we feel when we solve problems we see in other people instead of looking within ourselves.

We are quick to judge a person with a circumstance we have never encountered. It is easier, even convenient, to accuse and judge others than to examine our own issues.

I knew our church hosted a weekly Alcoholics Anonymous meeting and had heard stories of its incredible results. When a friend invited me to attend one night, I did so eagerly. Once there, I looked around and thought, "Yes, this is it! This is the perfect place, and these are the perfect people to minister to Luke. Finally!"

When the meeting ended, I called Luke to lay the groundwork for him to attend the next week's meeting. As luck would have it, he was scheduled to travel for work, but he agreed to come with me the week after that. I assured him I'd be with him, that he wouldn't have to attend the meeting alone.

Monday, the day of the meeting, I itched with excitement to call him. I needed to make sure he wasn't planning to skip out on it. We played phone tag all afternoon, but at last I nailed him down to a meeting time and place.

I spotted him and waved as he pulled into the parking lot.

The first words out of his mouth were, "I'm not gonna talk during the meeting—share, I mean."

"Okay. I have no expectations."

We sat and listened to many encouraging stories of triumph, of God's provision, of God's Hand of protection, and His incredible desire to redeem.

Out of the corner of my eye, I watched to see how Luke responded to each speaker and the testimonies, full of encouragement. There were tears in his eyes.

"I don't know how or why God loves me," said one man. "I just know that He does. I don't deserve His love. I've done so many horrible things. I've hurt many people. I don't deserve His grace. But He gave it to me. I don't deserve to draw another breath, but He sustains me."

My heart broke for Luke. He looked tired, burdened, his eyes glistening as he listened to all the stories of how great the Father's love is for us. After several years of a calloused heart, that night the callous in me softened and began to fall away. Compassion grew for him. When I saw his brokenness and sadness, I, too, felt tears well up.

For months I hadn't let myself cry about the addiction. Once the tears started that evening, a steady stream bathed my cheeks.

After a brief quiet period, I was startled when Luke cleared his throat and spoke, wiping away his tears with rough hands.

"Hi, I'm Luke. I'm an alcoholic."

"Hi, Luke!" everyone replied in unison.

"I wanted to say thank you to my sister for her invitation to come tonight. I'm blessed to have a sister who cares about me. I've spent years in a bad place. I'm not in a great place now. I want to get better. I don't want to keep hurting my family." He sniffed and grabbed a tissue. "I can relate to almost all of what's been shared here tonight. Thank you for what you said. It's good to be here."

"Welcome, Luke. Thank you for sharing," everyone said.

I hugged him.

"Thanks, brother. I'm glad you're here. And I'm glad to be here with you."

After the meeting we chatted with some of the folks before heading out.

"I'm proud of your bravery to speak up in front of the group," I told him as we walked to our cars. "And I'm proud of your honesty about where you are and how you feel. I hope it felt good to be here, to be surrounded by people who get it—supportive, kind people."

"I'm really glad you invited me," he said, hugging me. "When you called, I got annoyed. But I needed to be here, so thank you."

I smiled. "I'm elated you decided to come. And don't worry; I have no expectations of you. When you spoke tonight, it caught me off guard. I thought you weren't going to say anything . . ."

"I didn't plan on it, although I thought you'd probably want me to, but then something prompted me speak. I enjoyed tonight. I'm gonna come back."

My eyes widened.

Did he really just say, "I'm gonna come back"? Thank you, Jesus. That is what he said.

We hugged again.

I sat and watched as Luke drove away. My thoughts churned. *How will he get here next week? I'm gonna be out of town. Will he come if I'm not here? Will he come if I don't prompt him?*

That's when the Holy Spirit spoke to my heart.

God's got him.

God's got him.

"God's got him," I echoed.

And He did. And He does.

On the drive home, I prayed, "God, if You want him there, I know that You'll get him there. You've got him. You're more than able. You don't need me to meddle in his life. But Lord, I'm here. I'll help if You see fit, but I won't intervene unless I receive a clear word from You."

I repeated my prayer throughout that week. This was a test of sorts, to see whether I'd matured enough in faith to put my words into action. Did I really trust God to get Luke to the meeting? Did I really trust that Luke didn't need my help—and that if he didn't go, that God was still in control?

At 6:50 p.m. the next Monday evening, as I walked into a client dinner, my phone rang. The caller ID display read *Luke*.

"Hey, Steph, I wanted to let you know I'm on my way to the AA meeting."

My jaw dropped. I'd said God would get him there, but I still hadn't been sure. Luke had indeed gone without me, without me prodding or begging him.

"Call me later and let me know how it went."

I sat, distracted, throughout the evening as my clients talked and ate. I couldn't help it—I surreptitiously checked my phone every couple of minutes, afraid I'd miss his call. He called right before I went to bed.

"It was good," he said, his enthusiasm evident. "Thanks again for the introduction to the group. I enjoyed the people and the conversation."

Buoyant, I said, "That's great! I'm glad you made it back."

That night I learned a great lesson. God showed me He doesn't need me to orchestrate events. He has it under control. He needs me to stay in my lane and to pray and trust Him.

I fell asleep, on cloud nine.

❦

THAT INCREDIBLE LESSON allowed me to reflect on the many orchestrations, manipulations, and organized events I had been convinced Luke needed. Seldom, if ever, did I stop to ask if what I was doing aligned with God's plan for him. This lesson gave birth to a new humility in me and taught me that hands off was the best approach.

My old self would have fallen apart the week that followed, when Luke failed to return to AA. Doom and gloom would have eclipsed my world. My old self would have categorized his super-short stint in AA as an epic failure.

My new self, by contrast, viewed those two meetings he'd attended as a success. God spoke to me about how I lean on my own comprehension, and how I didn't trust Him to work things out. It showed me what is possible when faith is applied. It encouraged me to share God's intervention with others who struggle with the need to "do" something to help their addict. God is hands-on. His hand is easy to see when we are hands off.

READY. SET. PRAY.

"I CAN'T BELIEVE how excited I am to just chill, with nothing to do except to enjoy the movie and my time with you," I said, smiling affectionately at my husband.

"Yeah, it's been a long time since we've watched a movie. I hope this one's worth the time."

"Oh, I'm sure it is. Lots of the women at church say it's really worth a watch."

"Well then, let's hope they're right. You have the remote?"

We felt all too aware that our lives were running on empty. We really needed a night together, to sit and relax instead of think, to veg out and experience a feel-good movie, while fully aware that our spirits remained depleted. My hunger had grown for God, but I hadn't spent consistent time with Him. Time was a precious commodity, and using it to spend time with God didn't seem feasible or to fit in our already full schedule.

We chose the movie *War Room*, about a family that, from the outside, portrayed a picture-perfect

> *We felt all too aware that our lives were running on empty.*

life. Inside, however, the marriage was crumbling. Elizabeth, the wife, meets an older woman who, over time, teaches her the power of prayer, particularly when facing hefty life issues, and to pray with a clear-cut strategy during those periods when spiritual warfare persists.

When the movie ended, I sat motionless and stared at the screen as the credits rolled. We had just been handed a manual to improve our prayer life, quiet times, and overall effectiveness in life. The movie provided tools for rewriting our relationship with the God we professed to love but until this point had made little time for.

"So, what did you think of the movie?" Marshall asked.

In my sporadic quiet times, I would pray with sincerity, "God will You use me? I don't want to be in business for the sake of business. I want to work for You, with You, to carry out Your plan and purpose for me." And a call came that night, as I sat cross-legged on the couch. I grabbed Marshall's hand and squeezed it, the silly smile I wear when I have a plan or an idea on my face. My usefulness to God directly correlates to the priority I place on developing a deeper relationship with Him.

"I know what I need to do now. God's shown me what He wants me to do next."

I had heard His voice.

I would love to use you to do Kingdom work, but you barely know Me.

"I know You," I protested. "I've known You my whole life. All the Sundays, the Wednesdays, the Saturday prayer services—my whole life—has been spent inside the walls of Your church."

My child, you know of Me. You know about Me. But you don't yet understand My Heart. It's impossible for you to carry out My plans and purposes when you don't know My Heart.

I couldn't argue with that. I knew so much of my Christian walk, trying to check off each holier-than-thou box, as if the more I checked, the greater my value or the esteem I was held in. The checked boxes were, of course, about me, not about the heart of a holy God.

I prayed, "God, use me," but I needed to train myself to become usable. I had wanted to do His work without any preparation required. As a child, I had adored soccer and loved to play in the games, but I loathed soccer practice because of the cold weather and the policy of no potty breaks. The fast pace coupled with the opportunity to win trumped learning the mechanics of the dribble.

His way is full of trials and tests to ensure I'm ready for the plan and the path He's laid out. If only He would sprinkle fairy dust like Tinker Bell and *poof* all believers into awesome faithful men and women. We would stand tall, with puffed-out chests, fists on hips, feet spread, and a confident smile like veritable Samsons.

For me to be professionally successful, it took careful planning, being mindful of details, and time, effort, energy, sweat, and sometimes even tears. It took strategy, mentors, experts, and a team of high achievers. Patience, character, humility, honesty, integrity, and courage are all required to mature in faith as well. These skills are learned over time, some more easily than others, but they are all necessary to a mature faith.

In 2 Corinthians 1:3-4, we learn that what Christ suffered for us overflows into our lives in order for us to experience the Great Comforter. And we, in turn, can comfort those around us who suffer because we have been comforted. Like a waterfall, our banks fill up with Him; we overflow to those around us all that has been imparted to us through Christ.

We benefit when we devote time to develop a deeper relationship with God, like we do with any other relationship we nurture. He does not disappoint. It takes humility to fall on our knees before a most holy Savior. To bow before Him symbolizes our recognition of His lordship. My prayer for each of us is that we would hunger to spend so much time bowed down to get to know our King that calluses form on our knees. This posture reminds us who the center of the world is. On our knees, He lifts us up.

> *To bow before Him symbolizes our recognition of His lordship.*

After I saw *War Room*, my heart was convinced to make a change and begin to spend time daily with God. The next morning, I got up early in deliberate prayer, to read scripture and journal.

Exactly one month from the day I'd started my daily prayer time, God stopped me in my tracks. I was attending and working a trade show for our business sector when, that evening after the show, I joined a trusted supplier based in the Netherlands for dinner. For months we had discussed further integrating our companies, to the extent of a possible merger. We ate and reviewed a contract my team had put together, which laid out the best-case scenario for our business. As my eyes scrolled over the pages, I heard a voice speak to me, quietly yet clearly.

Stop. Don't go any further. It's time. It's your time to move on.

Startled, I looked up and scanned the room. Who'd said that?

Stop. It's your time to move on.

I tried to remain calm and composed as I considered those words so that Franz, my supplier, wouldn't see how rattled I'd suddenly become.

"Franz, I just remembered I have a whole lot of customer pricing requests I need to pound through tonight, before the show tomorrow. Let's pick this up tomorrow, okay? I think one more night to sleep on this would be good for both of us."

He looked at me, baffled. "I'm sorry; I don't understand. We're so close to the end of the contract. Why not finish?"

"I know, and I'm very sorry. I don't mean to bolt on you, but I can't put orders without pricing into our customers' hands."

Franz leaned back in his chair and studied me. He knew me well enough to know that my heart was never in the details of a project but always focused on the vision, the big picture. He knew a finished contract excited me ten times more than a price request.

I gave him an apologetic smile, scooped up my papers, and darted out of the restaurant, headed for my hotel room. As the door to my room shut behind me, I crumpled to the floor. On my face, before God, I wept and tried to get my mind around what His words meant.

"My time to move on? Move on to where? To what? Why now?" The questions poured out of me. "Did I hear You right, God?"

I prayed for God's direction, and just when I least expected it, He showed up. He cleared and corrected my path. On my knees that night I surrendered my will for His and felt the warmth of the Savior's arms envelop me like a heated blanket, surrounding me with a comfort and peace I could not explain.

Okay, God, I won't run from you. I'm yours. I'll do whatever it is You want me to do. Thank You for clarity tonight.

There have been only a few moments in my life when God has directly intervened and said, "This way. Follow Me." These are life trajectory moments of change.

I would have to share this one with my parents. I felt terrified, yet ecstatic. I had the clarity to move forward that God had given me, but I fretted about how my parents would react to the idea to sell the business I'd been managing the past few years for them.

As I unloaded my excitement, the profundity and unbelievable lightness I felt, there was silence on the other end of the phone as they considered what I was saying.

"I can't explain it," I said. "I just know we're supposed to sell the business. It's time for us to walk away."

After a few moments, Mom broke the quiet.

"All things work together for good." She paused. "You know, Dad and I contemplated selling once before."

"We know the long hours you work," Dad added, "and the travel you do for the company. We understand why you'd want to have more time with your family, more time with your girls. We want that for you, too."

"Let's talk through logistics when you return home from your trip," Mom suggested.

I laughed, delighted. "Wow, this went a lot more smoothly than I'd expected! I'll call you to talk more when I get home."

What just happened?

I felt more valued and validated as their child than ever before. They trusted me. They trusted my judgment. I had grown in my role as president and earned their respect. I wondered what everyone else's reaction would be. Surely, to walk away from the role of company president at age thirty and sell the business without another job to go to could be seen as insane. Certainly by my standards it seemed insane. But God had now wrought other plans for my life. He was calling me to a different purpose.

The first step toward God's plan was to show me how to be content without knowing precisely what it entailed and to trust Him with my life—our lives—when I had no idea what lay ahead, which direction I was about to move in. I couldn't trust Him with my loved ones' and friends' lives if I didn't first completely trust Him with mine.

That May, we sold the business and I moved on. Months passed with no further indication from God what I was meant to do beyond rest, be faithful in prayer, and trust Him. In the meantime, I interviewed with several great companies whose leadership and mission I could get behind. But I was repeatedly told that I'd be a great fit there, a good addition to their team, but that the timing wasn't right.

What timing? They needed the position filled and I was available. If it's such a good fit, why the holdup?

"God, why? Why will none of these positions pan out for me?" I cried out in frustration. "Why, when I am qualified, even overqualified? Nothing!"

It is I who make you qualified. Stop striving, Stephanie. Be still and enjoy this season of rest. You must learn to be content with the in-between.

Stop longing to have your need for a title filled. That is not who you are. You are Mine. You are My precious child. Find your identity in Me. What I need from you now is patience. Just wait. I have a plan and purpose for you. Wait.

"I hear you God, but I want to feel needed. I want to feel the excitement of problems solved and processes made better. I miss the office camaraderie. I want my title back. What do I call me now? I'm a nothing."

> *Stop longing to have your need for a title filled. That is not who you are. You are Mine.*

Serve your family. Spend time being healthy. And spend time with Me daily.

He gave a simple invitation to be still, rest, and participate in self-care. He invited me to discover His love, an invitation to see His purpose.

God stripped away things I placed value on to grab my attention, which left me no choice but to relent and offer my full attention to Him. It was time to surrender.

Dead ends and closed doors are as much guides for the future as open doors and open ends. This change demanded I recalibrate, that I shift from a constant state of scurry to one that allowed me time to breathe, take walks, and engage in early morning prayer and lots of heart and mind work in order to get comfortable in my new identity.

ᆭ

I CAN'T SAY that I'm thankful for addiction's presence in our family. But addiction's presence, and its repercussions, exposed a spiritual desperation that led me to uncover my need for God. Nothing, or no one else, could quench my spirit.

My faith journey grew stronger through these trials. Without them, I could not fulfill the purpose to write this book and be stretched by the possibility that my story could offer help to others who need to experience hope, peace, and freedom. On my knees in obedience, a surrendered life to His plan in prayer, I readied my ears to hear and respond, my life forever changed.

> *Addiction's presence, and its repercussions, exposed a spiritual desperation that led me to uncover my need for God.*

After the new year, I got serious about the creation of a "battle zone of prayer" that I'd learned about in the movie *War Room*. This battle zone is a dedicated location, mostly private, like a closet, papered with scripture that focuses on the most urgent prayer needs. Watching this movie and embarking on my new journey with God proved to be an incredible experience. A fresh season of hunger for God and restoration of my empty spirit had begun. The fundamentals changed for me in my walk with God as I started to pray scripture with intentionality.

I cleared out a section of my closet, found some old index cards left over from my college days, and for a week spent my morning quiet time on the floor of the closet, asking God to help me identify scripture that aligned with my family and the battles we currently faced. I wrote each one on an index card and taped them onto the closet wall. The battle zone of prayer is designed to be simple and didn't require me to buy anything. It was okay to make use of what was available. It wasn't about making it perfect, structured, or immaculate, just serviceable.

The scriptures I selected applied to each area of life that I found a struggle and where I needed to experience growth. My growth is a continual journey; I am still broken and in need of much work in these areas. But change took place in my life because of these verses and because of the prayers that went up to the heavens surrounding these verses. I know that for certain.

For myself, I prayed for contentment (Hebrews 13:5-6), for wisdom (James 1:5-8), to find delight in the Lord (Psalm 37:3-6), for perseverance (Romans 5:3-5), for stillness (Exodus 14:14), for hope (Isaiah 40:31), for restfulness (Matthew 11:28), to bear spiritual fruit (John 15:5), for increased desire for God (Psalm 143:8), to be a noble wife (Proverbs 31) and for living water of Christ to flow out of my life and onto those around me (John 7:37-38)

For Marshall, I prayed for his faith to increase to mountain-moving faith in Christ (Matthew 17:20) and that he would lead our family in faithful servanthood and teach us to have our foundation on the rock of the gospel (Matthew 7:24-26).

For Cora and Lydia, my sweet girls, I prayed the Beatitudes over them so that they will grow up to be women of Godly character (Matthew 5:3-11).

For our parents, I prayed that they would be encouraged in

their faith (Titus 2:1-15) and that Marshall and I would honor them even as adult children (Ephesians 6:2).

For Luke, I prayed that he would find delight in God and be rescued (Psalm 18:16-17 & 19), for freedom from his past (Psalm 118:5), that he would be built up in his faith (Hosea 6:1), and that he would experience an abundant life in Christ (John 10:10).

Each morning I would rise from bed, go straight to the serenity of my closet, and read verse by verse aloud, replacing the pronouns in them with my name or that of the person I was praying for. Then I would pray the scripture, reiterating it in my own words to convey a deeper, more pertinent meaning. The idea was to spend time meditating on each scripture to deepen my heart's understanding of His words.

The words of scripture are real and tangible. There is power behind The Word. The Living God was right there, in the closet with me, because I prayed His words, and Jesus is the Word made flesh. When my strength failed, I didn't worry because He never grows weary or tired. On days when I felt my energy fade, I got out of bed and went to my battle zone of prayer anyway, and He filled my energy bank. His strength became mine.

> *When my strength failed I didn't worry, because He never grows weary or tired.*

Much of human life feels like a battle, as if we are embroiled in an ongoing fight with no relief. Most days we fear we've lost a battle. This may or may not seem like good news to you, but you *are* in a battle over life and death. It is a daily battle with Satan over your soul.

Satan's mission is to deceive and trick us. He is crafty. When we are alone, tired, and feel weak, we are at our most vulnerable to Satan's attacks. He will do his best to get a foothold. Alcoholics Anonymous, or AA, and Al-Anon, the support organization for families of alcoholics, use the acronym HALT—which stands for Hungry, Angry, Lonely, and Tired—to indicate those times when we are most vulnerable or most easily tempted.

> *When we are alone, tired, and feel weak, we are at our most vulnerable to Satan's attacks.*

What helped me fight against Satan's attacks was Paul's letter to the Ephesians, which outlines a defense strategy to defeat his schemes with the armor of God. It is not a question of *if* he will attack, but *when*. God's armor is stronger than any fortified metal, tougher than any attack Satan can throw our way.

I end my daily prayer time with Ephesians 6:10–20, a prayer that beckons the armor into its ready state. The armor is brought into action, to work together with prayer. I visualize myself performing each action. I place the helmet of salvation on my head. I pick up the sword of the spirit and grip it tightly. I strap on the breastplate of righteousness. I step into the shoes of gospel's peace. And I slide my arm through the shield of faith. My defensive walls toward people—family, friends, co-workers, and any other humans in my path—go down. My defensive walls against Satan go up, reminding me that my war is not against flesh and blood but against the evil one.

Before we can suit up with God's armor, it's important to know who the enemy is and where the battle rages. With His armor we receive salvation, peace, righteousness, faith, and the Holy Spirit. We don all these attributes and they come alive with prayer. The enemy doesn't stand a chance when we suit up. God protects our minds, our hearts, our peace, our faith, our trust in the Holy Spirit's power. We pray because it is our defensive action against the evil one. We must discern who our true enemy is and fight the right battle, fully equipped with God's armor.

The Women's Ministry at church hosted a women's conference, where they presented Priscilla Shirer's Bible study, *Armor of God*. I arrived that Saturday morning right on time by my standards, admittedly late by most standards. All my responsibilities that wouldn't get done while I attended the conference lurked in my mind.

The woman at the check-in table greeted me. "Here's your folder with all of the conference and study information and your name tag."

"Better hurry in—they just started," another woman added.

I plopped into a seat in a row toward the back, the place where the latecomers sit and tossed my purse on the floor. I felt distracted, somewhat anxious, and agitated. The Women's Ministry leader was speaking as I settled in, but I heard not one word of what she said.

No, I am not going to spend the rest of this day in a tizzy.

I bowed my head and prayed, "God, you know I anticipated

good learning from this conference. Please remove the emotions and distractions from my mind and help me to focus attention on You. I pray that You pour Your peace on me right now and help me slow down. Help me to be present. Amen."

As I finished praying, the *Armor of God* video started. "Just because he's invisible," Priscilla Shirer narrated, "doesn't mean that he is fictional."

I know the devil's not fictional.

I thought to myself, *You know that he's real, but do you live your life as if he's fictional? Do you live your life as if others, people and circumstances, are your enemy? Do you even know who your enemy is?*

The video segment ended, and we broke into small groups for discussion on the lesson "Sizing Up the Enemy." My group of half a dozen discussed what stood out to us from the lesson.

"I don't know who the enemy is," I admitted. "I believe the enemy is anyone who makes me angry, anyone who challenges what I do or say. The enemy's the guy who cuts me off while I'm driving."

This was met with nods and grins.

"But if that's true," I continued, "then my kids are the enemy, as well as my husband, my mother-in-law, the stranger in the car, and on and on. I've made people, most of whom I love dearly, the enemy, when it's Satan who's the enemy."

It was true. I misplaced blame onto people. I held grudges and resentment. I walked around with a chip the size of a boulder on my shoulder. I kept people at a distance because I battled them and not the real culprit, Satan.

I kept people at a distance because I battled them and not the real culprit, Satan.

That conference proved to be a pivotal moment in my faith journey. Just weeks later, what I'd learned was put to the test when I found myself quarreling with my husband.

"I don't know how to explain myself any more clearly, Marshall. Why can't you just understand?"

"Can you explain to me what you're trying to accomplish again? Start from the beginning and I'll try to understand," he said patiently.

"I don't want to start over from the beginning. I want you to listen. If you listened . . ."

Your war is not against flesh and blood.

I stopped mid sentence upon hearing those words. My war was not against flesh and blood. I looked at Marshall.

"I want to stop this conversation. I'm not in the right frame of mind to continue, and I don't want to yell, I don't want to argue. Can we take a break and come back to it later?"

Startled by the abrupt change in my tone, he said, "Sure, yes, of course. I'm sorry I made you angry."

"And I'm sorry I yelled at you."

Such arguments were commonplace in our marriage, robbing us of hours of harmony and wrought hours of contention and relationship wedges. But now I'm more conscious of who I'm warring against, and I'm well equipped with the right armor to fight, to stop and think through who or what is causing tension and why.

Guess who's the culprit most often. Yep, it's Satan.

Today, my battle to wage war against addiction still simmers. Months of sobriety for Luke have given me hope, but this issue has by no means been laid to rest for us. We are a family ever fighting on God's side—His plans, His timing, His direction. We fight with prayer, not with action. Prayer illuminates the finish line. Prayer refills my hope tank. Prayer activates change.

> *Prayer refills my hope tank.*
> *Prayer activates change.*

JOY LIKE A TREASURE

MAX LUCADO WRITES in his book, *Great Day Every Day: Navigating Life's Challenges with Promise and Purpose*, "Worry is to joy what a Hoover vacuum cleaner is to dirt: might as well attach your heart to a happiness-sucker and flip the switch."

I have been the Hoover vacuum cleaner, and my worry so consumed me that it sucked the joy out of me and everyone close to me. Specks of joy were hard to find. For a worrier like me, one of the often overlooked verses in the Bible is Romans 12:12, which teaches us to be patient in trials, to be faithful in prayer, and to rejoice in the hope that we have.

It sounds incongruous to think about joyfulness in dark times, whereas the act of worry feels productive. Joy seems unproductive to our human minds.

I used to think that the only option available when undergoing a trial was to own up to a life of miserable sadness and depression, determined to be as miserable as the addict, to be as hopeless as the situation looked at face value. If I wasn't distraught, it meant I didn't "bear my brother's burdens," that I wasn't doing everything I could to help.

One Thursday afternoon in the fall of 2016, I walked into an Al-Anon meeting, discontentment

The act of worry feels productive.

on my sleeve, my mood black. God had stripped me of the full-time job that had created for me an identity I enjoyed. So I was upset at Him, at His choice for me not to work full time. I fought against learning to live in my new skin, in my new way of life. I pouted about it. I felt particularly irate that day. Nonetheless, I showed up to the meeting and sat with tightly crossed arms and legs, only half-listening, seething.

Toward the end, the facilitator passed around a two-by-three-inch daily calendar with inspirational quotes inside from Al-Anon participants and had each of us choose a page and read its message aloud. When it was my turn, I inwardly sighed, gazing at the serene photo on the cover page, the very antithesis of how I felt at that moment. I obediently flipped it open and read aloud: "I can still be happy, even if my alcoholic is drinking."

> *"I can still be happy, even if my alcoholic is drinking."*

I tore out the page, folded it in half and then in half again, and shoved it in my jacket pocket, the words echoing in my brain as I passed the calendar to the next person.

I sat, struck by the words that kept repeating inside my head. My hand moved to my pocket, stroking the paper with my fingers as if to absorb it through my skin, to let the meaning of it sink in to where I might come to believe it.

I looked around to see if anyone else had rejected or been puzzled by the statement I'd read. Instead, others were reading their papers, while I no longer listened. I saw nods, grins, and the occasional tears, tears of acceptance rather than upset.

What did I miss here? Did I come to the right meeting? Why do these people with so much to be sad about look so at ease and content?

I pursed my lips.

I guess these people are still living in denial, poor things.

When the share time ended, we rose from our chairs. Around me, people chatted casually. I made my way to the back door, still at odds with myself, pausing only when I felt a hand tap my arm. I recognized the woman as one of the group's facilitators.

"Hi, I'm Paula. I've seen you here before. I just wanted to introduce myself."

"Hi, I'm Stephanie, and that's very kind, but I'm kind of in a hurry. I've got errands to run and not much time to do them. You know how that goes, I'm sure," I added, forcing a smile.

"Well, we're thankful to have you and would love to see you again. Do you have any questions before you go?"

Are you kidding me? I have tons of questions. I just wouldn't know where to begin.

"Yes, actually, I do have a question," I said, the words tumbling out before I was even aware of them. I fished the paper out of my pocket and read it aloud again: "'I can still be happy, even if my alcoholic is drinking.' I don't get it. How can I be happy when there's so much pain, heartache, and worry alive inside of me? How on earth can I be happy when he doesn't want help?"

Paula reached out and took my hand.

"You have to first be open to the idea that it is possible to be happy, despite the circumstance. If you're open to it, then God will remind you of all you have to be happy about. Pray and ask Him. He'll show you."

When I got home, I read the words on that creased little piece of paper over and over, like I couldn't get enough of them. My heart was thirsty for this message. That "poor thing" who lived in denial—denial that life did not have to follow the tide of progress and setbacks—turned out to be me.

I needed consistency and stability. Instead I got wrapped up in the emotion of it all, unable to see truth. But as I read the words over and over again, I asked God to show me. How was it possible to find joy when someone I loved was in turmoil? The words from Romans 12:12 counseled me to be patient, to be faithful in prayer and rejoice in what hope there is, meant more to me now. Joyful and hope-filled, patient in affliction—I had tried so hard to adopt these characteristics, yet I possessed none.

I hadn't gone to that meeting to look for God, or anyone else for that matter, but I'm thankful that God showed up for me on that Thursday afternoon, through an Al-Anon meeting and a caring woman named Paula. He knew what I needed to hear, at exactly the right moment, to realign to His word. Despite having so much to be happy about, I'd let someone else's addiction rob me of my joy. And in doing so, I'd robbed others of their joy as well.

Self-indulgent misery is not worth it.

Self-indulgent misery is not worth it. What I think about, where my thoughts dwell—I have power over them; they do not have power over me anymore. I have been set free from the belief that hollowed eyes and being overcome with grief were my destiny until the problem was solved. Today I am more aware than ever that the addiction exists, and will continue to exist, and the wreckage of the past may never be healed or mended in totality on this earth.

Joy is developed over time, through repetition, like learning how to repeatedly throw a fast-pitch ball in the strike zone. Joy takes practice. It's a skill to be learned and honed. Joy bubbles up from the deep well of our souls.

It is not human nature to possess a peace-throughout-the-storm outlook on life. Every life challenge presents a new opportunity. God is faithful and reminds me that I do not have to carry a burden that is not mine to carry, and that He will always be with me to help carry the load. If He is with me, there is nothing more for me to worry about. He's got my back.

Search for joy like a pirate in pursuit of the most valuable of treasures. Follow the treasure map—the Bible—to be guided to where X marks the spot, where joy can be found.

Dictionary.com defines joy as "the emotion of great delight or happiness caused by something exceptionally good or satisfying; a source or cause of keen pleasure or delight." Where might we, as believers, find this kind of emotion—great delight; exceptionally good; satisfying? What is the source or cause for us to experience delight?

It is found in our God, Who loves us far more than we deserve, and in the sacrifice Jesus made so that we can now live in eternity, in utopia, the Eden that God created for us to experience. To live in the fullness of God's love and Kingdom. These ideas are sufficient to cause us to radiate with profound joy.

Search for joy like a pirate in pursuit of the most valuable of treasures.

In a June 2008 post titled "Why Do You Worry?" on the blog Living Proof Ministries, Beth Moore writes: "I've come to learn from God that worry is a waving red flag to the enemy. It is a dead giveaway that the person owning it does not trust God. The shield of faith is down. So fire when ready. Every time we're tempted to take it all on and worry something to death, let's say aloud from the depths of our souls, 'I choose to trust You, Lord. I choose trust. I choose You.'"

When you begin to worry, I urge you to stop and ask yourself: Who has robbed my joy? Sometimes it is the enemy, sometimes it is ourselves, in self-sabotage mode. We worry to the point that we are hard to be around, and others find it hard to relate to us.

I worried myself half to death. I believed that if Luke fell into trouble, I couldn't allow myself to experience any of the joys of life. No goodness. No peace. No happiness permitted. Worry numbed my spirit. Worry fizzled the spark of life. Worry wrecked hope. Worry took over, like weeds in a neglected garden.

Addiction as the circumstance, fear as the response, and perpetual worry became my identity. I stopped living in the truth of the Bible, which tells us not to be anxious. With a thankful heart, I confess God did not leave me there. He used Paula and Al-Anon as vessels to open my heart to see the depletion of joy, and how He longs to fill the void.

Like a slow, steady, singularly focused journey, there are stops along this new path, occasional wrecks, maybe even a robbery. But

> *Worry numbed my spirit. Worry fizzled the spark of life. Worry wrecked hope.*

my road is steady, immovable even, and strong. My new path is my Lord Jesus Christ. Before I found my new path, I had become a pawn to my own will.

My new road with Christ at times becomes overwhelming and emotional—I am a person, after all—but its foundation is not rocked. I am no longer ruled by those emotions but find joy in Him. My circumstance does not dictate my hope.

SOUL HEALING

"BURN THE BOAT, Stephanie," my good friend Abbe told me after I'd ranted my frustration at how easily I retreat to a comfortable, so-called Christian life. Faith, obedience, and soul-healing require risk, to get out of the boat, as Peter did, eyes focused on Christ, and step onto the waters of life. But my tendency is to poke one toe into the water and once I feel the rocking of the waves, before I know it, I've hopped back into the boat. How do I keep myself from withdrawing to my comfortable place where my faith is not stretched and my soul is not healed?

Abbe was right. I had to burn the boat.

Soul-healing happened for me during those times when I've allowed God to stretch my faith. The nineteenth century Scottish author and minister George MacDonald said, "You don't have a soul. You are a soul. You have a body."

In most cases, it's easier for us to care for our physical needs and neglect the soul's needs. Our soul's needs are less tangible. On the one hand, we will not physically starve to death if we do not care for our soul. On the other hand, the beauty of life, the taste of food, the everyday miracles, the twinkle in the stars—all these will go unnoticed if our soul is not well.

Soul rest and healing does not come of its own accord. Respite must be sought. It must be intentional. It must be located. Self-care is essential to maintain calm amid the storms of life. Time is needed to break away, to quiet the mind and ease the strain. Even though the world around falls apart, we can hold it together because we operate from inner peace. We operate out of composure and contentment.

The beauty of life, the taste of food, the everyday miracles, the twinkle of the stars—all these will go unnoticed if our soul is not well.

"Hush, little baby, don't say a word . . ." as the Graeme Revell lullaby goes—tranquility, calm. You can almost sense the sweetness of this moment as a mother rocks her little baby to sleep, comforts it with the gentle *hushhh*. That tender closeness warms our souls. The deepest part of us resonates with quietude. As our souls calm, we can evaluate scenarios and events around us with clearer intuition and reason. Stillness for our souls opens our minds to think anew, to dream anew, to experience life in abundance.

The absence of rest for our souls leaves our minds clouded and our decisions, wisdom, and perceptions groggy with mismanaged reactions. The benefits that come from soul repose are endless because it impacts the very way we make decisions, respond, and view the world around us.

My physical body and soul became lifeless scrawny waifs. As the president of a packaging company, I managed the components that kept it in motion all while I raised a family, took sales trips, and volunteered at church and a small group. I kept myself busy because it helped take my mind off Luke and my failure to make headway with him. Even with all the busyness of life, the idea of addiction winning invariably sneaked back into my consciousness to trump all that needed my attention—it was the one problem I could not solve.

⁓

IN EARLY SPRING a couple of years ago, I was invited to a women's retreat. I came up with every excuse under the sun about why I shouldn't and couldn't go. Relatively new to this church, I didn't know that many women and didn't know anyone there very well.

After several weeks of persistent invitations from the Women's Ministry leaders, Marshall said, "Steph, just go. You could use the time away. You really need this."

He was right. I did need it. I needed to be surrounded by women who could lift my drooping spirit.

The retreat was a couple of hours' drive from the church, so

I carpooled with several of the women. As we drove, each of us shared what was going on in our lives.

"Wow, I'm not the only one who's been dealt a crappy hand," one of us said after listening to a few stories. Tissues and tears were shared, and then my turn came.

I did my best to keep it superficial at first. I talked about the challenges involved in balancing work and family life. Then, like a fissure in a dam, the truth of my soul's condition emerged.

"I did not want to come on this retreat," I admitted. "I preferred to stay at home and wallow in pity. My husband convinced me to come."

Then, like a fissure in a dam, the truth of my soul condition emerged.

I took a deep breath. "The truth is, I'm a mess. I'm broken and tired, and my soul is in desperate need of a refresh. I need to be refreshed this weekend. I need to encounter God in a new way. I long to get raw and real with Him and with you women."

There was silence for a moment.

"Thanks for your vulnerability, Stephanie," one said.

"Yes, thank you, Stephanie," someone else echoed. "I, too, need a refresh and to feel the closeness of God again. I've pushed Him out and tried to do life my way over the last year or so, and it is definitely not working. I'm ready to do it His way again."

"Me too," another said. "I came because I wanted to experience God and gain wisdom from women who've walked this road ahead of me."

"Sounds like I'm not as alone as I'd thought," I said with a grin.

"Can we pray right now?" one of the women suggested. "Let's pray over the weekend, over our hearts and minds and any distractions that come our way.

"Lord, this car is full of four broken and needy women who seek to do life Your way. We pray a fresh outpour of Your spirit on us this weekend. Lord, will You open our hearts to receive what You have for us—through the lessons, the songs of worship, conversations over lunch or dinner, or late-night talks? Would you please come, Lord, and strengthen us with Your power today, right here, right now? In Jesus's name, amen."

For the first time, I felt excited to have come on this retreat, and the weekend proved to be fruitful for me. God once again exposed my weakness and made me strong.

One exercise had us try to define God as we see Him in one word. "What does He mean to you?" the facilitator asked.

She encouraged us to meditate on that one word and to see what would come of it for the remainder of the year. My word was *faithful*. Even now when I think about this word, my soul is refreshed. It symbolizes all that God has done for me and for the generations of believers that have gone ahead of me. The promise of eternity. The promise of no more tears, no more sorrow, no more pain. He always follows through.

What does He mean to you?

I encourage you to complete this same exercise. When you think of God, what comes to mind? What word or words remind you of Him? Is there one word that stands head and shoulders above the rest? When you find the word that speaks to you, meditate on it. Write it down on a Post-it and stick it on your dashboard, your bathroom mirror, the fridge. Tuck it in your wallet. Look it up in the dictionary. And search for scripture that contains your word.

Within my experience, God has used one word, *faithful*, to draw me back to Him, to quench the thirst of my soul, to refresh and replenish my spirit. He can do the same for you.

It's hard to feel all alone, like no one understands the extent of the grief you feel. What I have learned over the years, though, is that just because the people around me are not visibly acting or reacting, it doesn't mean they feel the grief any less. It could simply mean they made the choice not to become a victim of their emotions.

It's true that you can find good—find God—in any circumstance. But you must look for Him. He is there. My thoughts have changed: I no longer ask myself what I'm going to do and, instead, focus on what God is doing. It's made an incredible difference in my ability to see God at work—to rest and let God be God, to rest and let Him do the heavy lifting, to rest in faith and trust that God is working all things together for the overall good.

My church is home to both an AA and an Al-Anon group. Countless stories have been told inside the walls of its fellowship hall of miracles God has performed. The AA meeting offered at my church is open—anyone can attend and listen—and AA meetings are one of my favorite places to be on a Monday night.

Some might wonder why I don't find this depressing or dispiriting. While I admit I inevitably reach for the tissue box almost every time I attend, my tears stem from witnessing the grace of God. He has enacted miracles in the lives of many who sit around those square tables. The depth of faith moves in these individuals, who are passionate and pursue God Who raised them from the pit of Hell and brought them into His light. When one has been at death's doorstep, where death didn't look so bad, a turnaround story from there offers so much hope to those who listen.

One night a man told of how God met him on a rooftop.

"There I was, standing on the corner atop an eight-story building, cursing at God, blaming Him for everything wrong in my life. I was mired in alcoholism and drug addiction. I desperately wanted to stop using, and ending my life seemed easier than going through detox again because it'd failed before. I didn't believe I could stop. I didn't believe my life was worth anything or that anyone would miss me. I felt I was doing everyone a favor. I'd been hateful to everyone around me and made life miserable for my family and friends."

He paused and rubbed the back of his neck, a look of disbelief on his face, as if he still couldn't believe what had happened that day.

"That same God I was cussing and cursing, and blaming for all the trouble I'd caused, met me on a city roof, eight flights up, as I lifted my foot to step off the edge."

You could hear the intakes of breath on hearing how he had almost ended it all.

"I was about to step off the ledge when God showed up, at the right place, at the right time. I heard a voice, so soft and gentle yet so clear and arresting: *Go home,* the voice said to me. *Go home,* it repeated.

"God showed His grace to me that night—me, a miserable sinner, a man who cussed at Him and told Him how much I hated my life. Before that moment, I wasn't even convinced God existed. But after that moment, there was no more doubt in my mind."

> *When one has been at death's doorstep, where death didn't look so bad, a turnaround...offers so much hope.*

Someone at the table said, "God isn't offended by our language; He's big enough to handle rejection. Even when we reject God, He extends His grace to each of us."

Another man spoke up. "I had a similar experience. I was about to take my own life when I heard God's voice so clearly. He assured me that if I put the gun down, He would help me get sober, and I knew I could do it with Him beside me, every step of the way. I also knew it was hopeless without Him."

Another gentleman told of his encounter with Christ, also on a rooftop as he was poised to end his life.

Stop, God said to him. *Go to your AA meeting and we'll figure this out together.*

Another met God in a cold, vacant warehouse in the middle of winter after a days-long binge.

We heard thirty minutes of story after story of God's voice, God's prompts, God's engagement with His creation—even when they hadn't been looking for Him. The stories soothed my soul. They helped my faith soar to higher heights and shake away my fears and doubts. It took courage for these men and women to share their conversion stories with individuals—strangers—who might not share their beliefs, courage to admit to themselves that God saw them as worthy of saving. One man remembered thinking, "He couldn't be talking to me. I've done too many bad things. I'm beyond saving."

It took . . . courage to admit to themselves that God saw them as worthy of saving.

We are never beyond the reach of God's grace. When there's nowhere else to turn, Jesus waits for us. Miracles happen, as I have seen and heard with my own eyes and ears. If you are in a place of doubt, where this kind of miracle seems like nothing more than a fairytale, one you would never expect to happen to your family, I encourage you to seek support. Attend an open AA meeting, or Al-Anon, or Celebrate Recovery, where you can find encouragement and support and create accountability for yourself, all of which are integral to personal healing.

We are wounded by addiction. Whether or not we are keen to admit it, we morph into a new persona to play Mr. Fix-it, counselor, adviser, judge, prosecutor, or victim. We hurt, and we hurt others. Surround yourself with people who get it, who understand where you're coming from because they've been down that same path before you. It can help to keep your mind, heart, and persona in check.

I sought support from women in AA, women on the road to recovery by God's grace. I heard a gentleman once say, "Relapse is not inevitable when God is in control, but relapse will surely get us if we are in control." The fact that some of these friends have been clean and sober for twenty-plus years is a testament to God's faithfulness and that miracles are possible.

These women have become an incredible source of support for me. They help me to understand, or at least see more clearly, the mind of the addict. Support like this is available to anyone, but we must be willing to take steps to find it. Not every group might work for you; it may take time to find the right fit, but the right fit is out there.

Stories of transformation cause me to fall on my knees with thankfulness that God's love for each of us is profound. In the life stories of these individuals, God has used sickness, kids and grandkids, tragedy, loss of all that seemed meaningful, and more. They would tell you that what they thought mattered back then—the next sales goal, fame, success, the next buzz—they count as loss now for the sake of a relationship with Jesus. What happens when we reach our goal, only to find the same emptiness we felt before?

As we walk along this road of family addiction, we can find ourselves trapped in loneliness. That is why it is critical to have support, people who can call your bluff, who can talk you off the ledge, who can speak to your life in ways the average friend cannot, and remind you of the miracles.

As we walk along this road of family addiction, we can find ourselves trapped in loneliness.

It is far too easy, as family members or friends of addicts, to convince ourselves that we aren't the ones who need help because we're not the ones with an addiction. However, we do need help, because we can't siphon the barrage of emotions that weigh us down. Our inability to process emotions on our own is why we thrive as part of community. We are meant to be surrounded by people who care about us, who understand us, and who can shine a light on miracles we might otherwise miss.

GRATITUDE'S LEAD
INTO ABSOLUTION

ANYTIME WE GET A CHANCE, my dad and I like to go for walks together. We usually walk early in the morning before anyone else is up. This has been our tradition since my college years when I spent summers at home. Back then, he would bribe me with the promise of a stop at Starbucks at the end.

One morning on our normal path around Lake Alpine, we reminisced about my childhood, trading highlights.

"I wonder how much Mountain Dew I consumed during softball season at the park every summer?" I mused.

My dad laughed. "That was before we knew soda was bad for you."

"Remember how Luke and I loved to race our bikes around our block? And how about all those times we finagled ice cream twice in one day without you knowing, once with our babysitter and then again, later, with you and Mom," I said, grinning.

"You cheater!" he exclaimed, chuckling. "Well, at least you had to walk there and back each time. Hey, what about all the ground balls and pop flies I made you catch with the pitching machine?"

"Oh, I loved that! Anything to be outside and run around and get dirty."

After an hour, we headed back home for breakfast, my mind flooded with wonderful childhood memories. I thought about how well Luke and I had played together—games of catch on the front lawn, Mario Bros. on the original Nintendo and Basketball Horse, riding our bikes to Shuey's Candy Store, watching hours and hours of *Dukes of Hazzard* VHS tapes, and playing countless backyard soccer games. The memories were endless, and I'd go back if I could in an instant.

It's easier to remember the struggles, the bad stuff that happened. I reached a point in my life where unpleasant circumstances consumed me, and I forgot where I came from. Intentionality is required to remember the good experiences. I'd forgotten the fun and laughter, the good memories. Over time, I'd grown bitter and unappreciative.

Not one bone in my body expressed gratitude for the current state of the family. From my perspective, how could I? Our existence was threatened by the quicksand that addiction creates. Yet when I took a moment to thank God for those beautiful, fun family memories of yesteryear, only then could I see my situation through a rosier lens. I wasn't happy about the situation we'd found ourselves in, but the blessings that were present were now visible.

I'd forgotten the fun and laughter, the good memories.

Most important, I could be grateful for Luke—I *am* grateful for Luke. When I focus on who he is, there is no fear. I applaud him for who he is: for his heart, which is kind and generous; for his love of '60s and '70s classic rock; for his love of comedies, especially satire; for his impeccable memory for sports, cars, baseball players, movies, TV, and history—any fact and he can retain it. And anytime there's a trivia night, he's everyone's first teammate pick.

Gratitude by its very nature uplifts. Gratitude frees my mind from whatever current woe has arisen and illuminates the years of countless provisions and faithfulness God has provided me. Gratitude sets my gaze on Heaven, so I don't get stuck on what exists only on earth. Gratitude leads the way, like an appetizer before the main course, to forgiveness.

Blessings are all around us. Luke is the only blood brother I have on this earth, and that is even more reason for me to be grateful for him. God paired us here as brother and sister. I have a role to play in his life—and it is not to save him. I have a role to play that no one else can play, including to be his sister, a connection that no one else on the planet gets to have with him. How often I have taken that position for granted.

⤳

EARLIER IN THIS BOOK, I shared a close encounter with God on a drive home from work. In those moments God addressed my immature use of words with his statement, *You pray for Me to be gracious to your brother, but you do not extend to him the same grace which you expect from Me.* He confronted my misaligned words

> *Gratitude leads the way, like an appetizer before the main course, to forgiveness.*

and heart, a dissonant-like violin practice for the novice. Using words, I sang praises to God, asked for mercy, grace, love, and protection to be showered on Luke, all the while, in the next breath, my heart cursed him. That dissonance bred a spiritual dual-personality disorder.

Saying rude words with a pleasant voice doesn't make the words any less offensive or harmful. It is not the volume of the words that got me into trouble but the words themselves. My tongue caused a lot of relational damage and left casualties in its wake.

I am now convinced that three little words act like a salve on an open wound, holding within them the power to heal: *I am sorry.* Apologies, when we make boneheaded comments, pave the way to a better relationship. Apologies, when we jump to conclusions and blame, open the door to restoration. Apologies, when we accuse and when we are self-absorbed and resentful, build tributaries of peace.

Dictionary.com defines *apologize* as an effort "to make amends for former misdoing, express remorse, regret" and offers the description "get down on knees." To kneel shows humility. When a person chooses humility on bended knee to someone they have offended to ask for their forgiveness, reparation begins.

The choice is simple: we can let pride win and ignore the change that we need to make, or we can embrace the change with humility and be grateful that God has presented us the opportunity to mend a broken relationship. When we apologize, it releases us from the bondage and control of our words. We are free to start again.

If you were to think back over your lifetime to the people you have known, who would you point out as the wisest? The wisest among us are those who are good listeners. They listen first before they speak. They speak with thoughtfully chosen words—and avoid blurting unconscious thoughts. They are mindful of word choice. Each word carries meaning. If it did not, it would not need to be said.

The wise speak with thoughtfully chosen words—and avoid blurting unconscious thoughts.

James 3:2 (NLT) says, "Indeed, we all make many mistakes. For if we could control our tongues, we would be perfect and could also control ourselves in every other way."

My grandmother and mother would admonish us with, "If you don't have something nice to say, don't say anything." Somewhere along the journey to adulthood, we have forgotten this little gem of wisdom. We believe our college degrees, years of business experience, years of teaching Sunday school give us a free pass to express whatever is on our mind without a filter. Regardless of how our words will be received, we believe that as we age, we have earned the right and have the authority to speak them.

Our subconscious mind thinks our voice needs to be heard to validate our existence and purpose on the earth. We crave words worth saying, snappy wisdom to share, and solutions to offer. The challenge we face is that our desire is to be known for our wisdom, but when we overuse offering it, it makes everyone around us who would otherwise benefit from our (God's) wisdom deaf to our voice. Too much of a good thing is just as detrimental as remaining silent when prompted to speak.

A fine balancing act is required of us if we want God to use us. He will guide our thoughts, our words, our actions, and our hearts. The challenge here is that we must let Him lead. Our concern is for Him to receive the glory for imparting His wisdom to us, for the solutions we come to, the creativity we display, the provision all around us. He is a trustworthy God. We fail daily, hourly. He never fails. He is perfect in every way.

Pride blinds us to true motivation. No matter what the circumstance, the names, the faces, to swallow our pride and say those three little words, "I am sorry," can transform our lives. Often as believers, we tend to put Christians on pedestals. We see religiosity as a caste system, legalistic and rigid. The righteousness we seek, to become more Christlike, breaks down any pedestal beneath our feet.

Apologies are a great way to demonstrate that we recognize our humanness and call to Christlikeness. Lines of communication cross at times, and in our effort to show that we long for a different life for our loved one, it often translates as, "You need to live a holy life, like mine," "I am up here, while you are down there," and "I have it all together; you are a muddy mess." We create a great divide: the us-and-them crevasse.

The righteousness we seek, to become more Christlike, breaks down any pedestal beneath our feet.

We are sinners saved by grace, not by our own works but because we accepted a gift Christ gave to us. Salvation is not a gift of entitlement or an invitation to begin construction on our holier-than-thou pedestals. Salvation is an invitation to humility, so that He is lifted high.

When I confronted Luke with unkind and judgmental words, I felt justified in my approach. My subsequent encounter with God in the car, as I drove home from work, made the grossness of my offense painfully evident. The need to apologize became great. When I told Luke, "I'm sorry I hurt you," I felt released. My heartbeat slowed.

Salvation is an invitation to humility, so that He is lifted high.

Forgiveness helps us to also gain a deeper grasp of the absolution we have been given through Christ. When I understand who I am considering the Creator God, it helps me put apologies into perspective. My war is not against my flesh and blood; it is against spiritual forces. Unforgivingness allows Satan to gain a foothold in our life, a foothold created because of our failure to be obedient to God's word.

One evening I sent Luke an email that told of my need for his forgiveness.

Today may you be reminded . . . how deep is God's love for you. His love is demonstrated in this—it was MY sin that nailed Christ to the cross and it was because of MY sin that Christ died so that we could be reunited and be made spotless before God. Also, I want to apologize if I have made you feel less than how God sees you. If I have made you feel guilty or condemned, I am sorry. That is not my intent, but I am human, and I, too, sin against my brother. Forgive me for being impatient with you and for not loving you as I should.

Respect and love for my one and only brother returned as intentionality grew in my need to apologize to him and my gratitude for him. An apology proffered reveals humanness and a desire to rebuild the relationship. It breaks down barriers. It opens—or reopens—the door to opportunities that would have been lost without admission of wrongdoing. Regardless of whether the words or act appeared justified, what matters is the cross now laid down to bridge the crevasse between us and them. Clear the air, wipe the slate clean, and start fresh with a grateful heart open to a better relationship.

RECONCILIATION

A COUPLE OF YEARS AGO my family threw a surprise ninetieth birthday party for my grandfather. I will never forget his face when he walked into the room. It lit up, and he raised his hands in disbelief. Tears welled up in his eyes as he gazed at his two sisters, one older and one younger. They hugged and cried tears of joy. It was priceless.

That is what I long to have with my brother, a tender heart of love, comforted by a bond that can't be broken. Now, just two years later, only one of the three siblings is still alive. I can only imagine the joy she will have when she reaches Heaven and rejoins her beloved siblings.

Their relationship gives me hope, because I know that God can heal relationships, and I have seen the miracles He has performed in people around me. I know it is possible for Luke and me, too. I'm not blind to the fact that my actions and choices marred relationships with my brother, my other family members, and even friends. And I'm quite certain there is a level of guilt that Luke carries as well. I pray for my relationship with Luke, that God restores us to an even better place than our childhood.

I would love to assert that my relationship with Luke is far better than it used to be. But it's not. And I don't know what to do with that fact. I want more than anything to have a brother, a sibling to share life with, to have my back on days that are rotten and fall apart. But I don't know if that's in God's plan for us.

I wish this part of our journey offered more success or wisdom to share. But it is my sincere hope that you might learn from my mistakes and not let your confrontation and desire for control damage your relationship with your son, daughter, brother, sister, or whomever you are worried sick over. Keep in mind, individual healing comes before relational healing is set in motion.

When we speak in a dialect of love, acceptance, mercy, grace, kindness, and peace, we pluck at heartstrings. Our culture is charged with hate, with identifying differences instead of focusing on unity. Anger and dysfunction plague every home and relationship. Kindness appears to be headed for extinction. As believers, we are called by God to do our part. Kindness knocks people off their game, because they don't expect to receive kindness in any form.

Kindness can wield a dramatic impact on those who believe they are not worthy to be shown goodness. Perhaps they feel they do not deserve kindness because of the hurt they have caused others or the life choices they have made. They believe they have earned hardship, hurt, and animosity. The olive branch of peace that we hold out to someone who has hurt us, wronged us, or even just made poor choices that affect us breaks down barriers and heals hurts—even when we don't get an apology in return.

When we speak in the dialect of love, acceptance, mercy, grace, kindness, and peace, we pluck at heartstrings.

In Matthew 25:23–24, we are told to be reconciled to the one we have offended before we can present an offering to God. My mind immediately demands to know who's at fault. Who started it? He said . . . or she said . . . My mind thinks, "I have a right to be offended."

The longer the hurt goes unreconciled, the harder it is to overcome the pride required to extend the olive branch of peace. And in the meantime, offerings to God carry an unpleasant aroma because they are rotten with pride.

The Bible doesn't give permission to hold grudges, and the Bible doesn't give us free rein to make our offenders pay for what harm we feel they've caused us or our family. The Bible does tell us, however, to forgive, and in doing so, we will also be forgiven.

The Bible, in Exodus 14:14 (NIV), offers to us another promise: "The Lord will fight for you, you need only to be still." Leave God's job as righteous judge and defender of His people to Him. Judge and jury are not in our job description as children of the Holy King—as much as we might like them to be.

Jesus gave His life so that we might be reconciled to God. He took on our sins—past, present, and future—and nailed each one to the cross. We have no accuser, because Satan, who accused us, has been cast into Hell. Defeated, he has no power over us.

The Greek word for reconcile, *diallasso*, means to change. According to the Blue Letter Bible, it means "to change the mind of anyone, to renew friendship with one." Any form of reconciliation requires change, not inertia or stagnation. Change can be hard. It's scary. Change creates vulnerability, especially when we're required to change our own thought patterns and behaviors. Reconciliation requires that we let go of the right we believe we deserve to hold a grudge and instead forgive.

I journaled this prayer a few years back: "Lord, Your love is not conditional or based on good works. Your love is condition-less, and that's what makes it so powerful. Consistently, with Your arms wide open, You welcome us back, You forgive, and You never hold a grudge. You say in Your word that You cast our sin away as far as the east is from the west, never to be remembered again. I pray You forgive me, Lord, for the times that I have failed to love as You love, when I hold a grudge, and how often I'm not willing to forgive. Transform our family that we would truly understand the meaning of unconditional, arms-wide-open love."

God is about reconciliation. He does not long for broken relationships; He longs for restoration. I knew the truth of God's word but got hung up in my own loophole of broken thought. I knew that I should show love and kindness to everyone, but if I showed love and kindness to Luke, I thought it would appear as if I accepted or condoned his behavior. The words *it would appear* are the proof that I got stuck in a lie. I understood the big picture—love and kindness—but got hung up in the implementation of both.

The gap in my thinking closed through God's work in my heart to show me what my own sin cost Him and the awesome price that He paid for me on the cross. The more I've become aware of my need for kindness, love, and mercy, the more I want to offer those gifts to others.

To love someone with grace, we must first understand the depth of the grace that we've been given. God doesn't play favorites. His gift of grace, "unmerited favor," is not available based on performance or lineage, location, economic or social class, or even church attendance. The grace that He offers is free—no exclusions, no gimmicks, no catch. Unmerited favor. You cannot, you did not, earn God's favor. And what's more, you cannot live beyond the reach of His grace. No matter how far you've run, no matter how close to the edge you've gotten, His grace can meet you there. All He needs from you is your permission. He will not push himself on you. He is kind.

> *You cannot, you did not, earn God's favor.*

Psalm 103 (TM) says, "it's in Christ that we find out who we are and what we are living for." My heart is open to the possibility that I can experience the fullness of God's grace, not merely crumbs of grace. I decided to embrace fully God's grace for me. It took time to be still before Him and let Him love me. It took time to be grateful for the gift of loving kindness and His heart for reconciliation. I made time to be open to changes in my heart, surrendered parts of me that needed to be healed, let Him comfort and soothe my heart with the balm of His grace. As the Lord began to minister to my heart and helped me to see and experience His grace more fully and understand the price He paid for me, it became easier for me to begin to share grace with others in my life.

> *My heart is open to the possibility that I can experience the fullness of God's grace, not merely crumbs of grace.*

The good old "pick yourself up by the bootstraps" mentality is not a helpful or effective sentiment. It is a reflection that we do not possess the wisdom of God to understand the grace that could be extended.

Time in God's presence helps us recognize the awe-inspiring power of His goodness. God did not want life apart from us, so He made a way that we could be reconciled—*diallasso*—to Him, through Jesus. God's desire and design include reconciliation. The deeper I understand this truth, the more equipped I am to be thoughtful in speech and recognize my role in restoration. Today I extend an olive branch of peace and get ready for the day, to wait with expectancy for the day, when my brother will reach out and grab it.

"MOM, YOU'RE LATE. It's 8:30. Time for devotions."

At Cora's words, I glanced at my watch.

"Oh, my goodness, this morning is flying by."

"Can I find the page we're on, Mama?"

"Of course you can!" I replied, smiling at Lydia. "Cora, will you read from your devotion book for us this morning?"

Cora opened her book, *Jesus Calling 365 Devotions for Kids*.

"'Have you ever climbed a mountain, a steep hill, or a rocky slope?'" she read. "'The climb is sometimes easy and sometimes hard. But all along the way I've prepared gifts for you—like flowers in the cracks of the rocks. These gifts might be special friends, happy days with people you love, or a chance to help someone else. They remind you that I am with you. Enjoy My gifts and enjoy traveling with Me. The climb isn't always easy, but the view is heavenly.'"

She stopped and looked at me.

"Thanks, sweetheart," I said. "Let me pray for you before you head out to school.

"Father, we thank You that You are always with us. Thank You for the blessings that You've planted along the route of our journey to know You. I ask today that You be with Cora and Lydia at school. I ask that You give them favor with their teachers and friends. I pray for Your protection over their hearts, minds, ears, eyes, and bodies. God, I pray that You give them the courage to be Your light at school today. Help them to show kindness and compassion to those around them. Help them to display Your love, so others will come to know You. In Jesus's name, amen."

In the parenting series *House or Home?*, Chip Ingram says, "You can't impart what you don't possess." And I would further say that you *do* impart what you *do* possess. In my lowest days of hateful words and easy anger, I bestowed bitterness and animosity on those around me. Today, by God's grace, we abide by these family rules: In our family we have faith, believe in grace, trust in God, expect miracles, give thanks, pray always, love one another, and choose joy.

My ascent to hope, toward a deeper, more intimate relationship with Jesus, continues. As I look down the paths behind me,

I can see my greatest treasure along the way was to bring people with me. My changed life, my steps of obedience, like a ripple on water's surface, was a chain reac-

> *My changed life, my steps of obedience, like a ripple on water's surface, was a chain reaction.*

tion. My girls' and my husband's faith and hope have grown to embrace frequent prayer and daily time with God. Why? Because they saw the change in me. A life reconciled to Jesus is thrilling and contagious, and this life is only the beginning.

DISCUSSION QUESTIONS

PART 1: THE AVALANCHE

1. How would the journey through addiction be different if undergone apart from Christ?

2. What expectations have you held on to that you need to let go?

3. What one step can you take to begin to let go of the expectations you have of your loved one and his or her recovery?

4. What role have you played with your addict or alcoholic?

   a. codependent

   b. enabler

   c. savior

   d. rejecter

   e. judge and prosecutor

   f. detective

5. How has your role damaged your relationship with your loved one? Or has it? How could your relationships and reactions be improved?

6. How has the presence of alcoholism and addiction in your family impacted your health?

7. What is one change that you can make to participate in self-care? (Examples might include exercise, massage, taking walks, meditation, yoga, having coffee with a godly friend.)

8. What has God been prompting you to do that you're afraid to do?

9. Have you considered that responding in obedience not only is designed to help others but has the power to change you as well?

10. When you think about walking in obedience to Christ, what comes to mind?

11. What holds you back from responding to His prompts?

12. Have you experienced a breaking point? Are you ready to stop being in charge and let God be in charge?

PART 2: FROM FEAR'S GRIP

1. What fears are you holding on to?

2. What thoughts rob your sleep? What Bible verses could you use to replace those thoughts?

3. In the same way I used busyness, what do you use to mask your hurt and pain?

4. What do you wish to control?

5. What are some of the what-if's you're carrying around? Can you find the courage to share your worries with a trusted support person and ask them to pray with you about them?

6. On the days when you feel utterly hopeless, what do you do to persevere and push through?

7. What behaviors do you need to stop or change?

8. What trust have you broken due to manipulative actions?

9. Do you see your loved one as stained and labeled? What are some things you can do to change your perspective on those stains and labels?

10. Are you allowing busyness to overshadow your unaddressed pain?

11. How do you manage, or not manage, the emotional highs and lows?

12. Fear can be paralyzing. What fears do you need to face head on and hand over to God for Him to help you release?

PART 3: TO FAITH'S SUMMIT

1. What boundary lines have you crossed?

2. What boundaries have you laid?

3. What boundaries do you need to lay?

4. Do you believe God has your loved one in His hands?

5. What verses encourage you to have faith despite the storm?

6. From whom do you need to ask forgiveness?

7. What do you need to let go and forgive yourself for?

8. How would you describe your prayer life? Are you ready and willing to dive into prayer?

9. What are you grateful for in your life and in your loved one's life?

10. Do you believe that reconciliation is a part of God's plan for us? If so, whom do you need to seek reconciliation with? Is something holding you back from reconciling?

11. Do you believe that miracles happen today, even when your situation seems bleak?

12. Do you believe that joy is a state of being that you can obtain? Do you believe that God wants you to find joy? How will you seek out joy in the coming days, weeks, and years?

ABOUT THE AUTHOR

STEPHANIE WINSLOW, founder of Blind Spot Consultants and co-founder of New Dominion Healing Center, is first and foremost a pursuer of Christ. *Ascent to Hope: The Rugged Climb from Fear to Faith* is her first book.

An organizational change agent, Stephanie has helped nonprofit and for-profit organizations develop and implement strategic plans, develop training systems, and improve overall business processes with a focus on employee development.

Stephanie graduated from Ohio Wesleyan University, with degrees in Spanish and education. She also has a MA degree in higher education from Geneva College. Stephanie holds a Lean Six Sigma Certificate and is certified as a faith and health ambassador.

Stephanie lives in Saint Louis, Missouri, with her husband, Marshall, an IT consultant for the health-care industry, and their two daughters. She enjoys coffee, trail running, yoga pants, and spending time with friends and family. She volunteers weekly to cook for the families of her church. Together, Stephanie and Marshall also enjoy traveling, DIY projects, dance parties, and craft time with their girls.